Outstanding Dissertations in

ECONOMICS

A Continuing Garland Research Series

Aspects of Efficiency in a Socialist Developing Country: Iraq

Victor C. Levy

Garland Publishing, Inc.
New York & London, 1984

Library of Congress Cataloging in Publication Data

Levy, Victor.
Aspects of efficiency in a socialist developing country, Iraq.

(Outstanding dissertations in economics)
Originally presented as the author's thesis (Ph.D.—University of Chicago, 1978) under title: Aspects of factor productivity and economic efficiency in a socialist developing economy.
Bibliography: p.
1. Industrial productivity—Iraq—Mathematical models.
2. Efficiency, Industrial—Iraq—Mathematical models.
I. Title II. Series.
HC415.4.Z9I525 1984 338'.06'09567 79-53642
ISBN 0-8240-4161-5

All volumes in this series are printed on acid-free, 250-year-life paper.

Printed in the United States of America

THE UNIVERSITY OF CHICAGO

ASPECTS OF FACTOR PRODUCTIVITY AND ECONOMIC EFFICIENCY IN A SOCIALIST DEVELOPING ECONOMY

A DISSERTATION SUBMITTED TO
THE FACULTY OF THE DIVISION OF THE SOCIAL SCIENCES
IN CANDIDACY FOR THE DEGREE OF
DOCTOR OF PHILOSOPHY

DEPARTMENT OF ECONOMICS

BY

VICTOR C. LEVY

CHICAGO, ILLINOIS

AUGUST, 1978

ACKNOWLEDGMENTS

I would like to thank the members of my thesis committee, Professors Arnold C. Harberger, Arnold Zellner and Dennis W. Carlton, for their assistance and invaluable help in the process of writing this dissertation. Throughout the period of this research, Professor Zellner's continuing guidance, questioning and encouragement were greatly apprecaited. Professor Harberger and Professor Carlton have given generously of their time in reviewing my work and offering suggestions for improvement.

Financial support during the course of my graduate study and the conduct of this research at the University of Chicago has been provided by a Lily Honor Fellowship and a National Science Foundation grant, number SOC 7305547.

Last, but not least, I would like to extend my gratitude and appreciation to my wife Elana and my daughter Addie for their encouragement, understanding and patience. Also, I would also like to extend my gratitude to my parents who provided me with the stimulus of learning.

TABLE OF CONTENTS

LIST OF TABLES

INTRODUCTION

This dissertation consists of three essays dealing with the theory and measurement of total and specific factor productivity and various aspects of economic efficiency. Iraq, a socialist developing economy, is used as a case study.

There are two distinct approaches to study the relative contributions of factor inputs and technical progress to economic growth. Chapter I develops and uses the Divisia index approach to study the relative contributions of capital accumulation, labor input growth and total factor productivity to the growth of the industrial sector in Iraq.

Since the 1958 change in government in Iraq, the public sector has been assigned a greater role in pursuing economic development and industrialization than the private sector.[1] Since 1960, public investment in Iraq has been more than three quarters of total investment. We thus analyze the relative importance of factor input contributions and non-factor contributions to growth in the private and the public sectors in the years 1960-67. Special attention is given to the massive expropriation of private firms by the government in 1964 and its effect on the growth of factor productivity in both sectors.

In pursuing the Divisia index approach, we assume (1) that the production function is characterized by homogeneity of degree one (constant returns to scale) and (2) neutral technical change. We further assume (3) that the payments to factors of production are made according to their marginal

---

[1]Many other middle eastern countries have assigned to the government the role of directing and implementing economic growth and development. Egypt, Iraq, Jordan, Kuwait, Syria and Turkey have used periodical development plans during the 1960's. In each case the public sector was expected to play the major role in implementing them. Particularly striking is the dominance of planned public investment in the agricultural and industrial sectors.

productivities. Intuitively, one feels that there are many cases in which such simplifications might give biased results. Specifically, it is easy to challenge the third assumption in the context of a socialist economy such as Iraq.

In Chapter II we develop a parametric approach to the analysis of total and specific factor productivity and apply it to the public manufacturing sector of Iraq. The contribution of the parametric approach is that it does not rely on the assumption of constant returns to scale. Non-neutral technical change is modeled, estimated and linked to the conventional average input specific productivity indices. Using duality theory, the parametric approach is derived with a restricted profit function, dual to the production function, which allows for the capital service input not to be paid the value of its marginal product. The parametric results are compared with results of the Divisia analysis presented in Chapter I. During the period of the analysis, the share of labor in value added dropped from 0.387 in 1961 to .267 in 1967, i.e., a drop of 41.6 percent in a period of just seven years. Furthermore, the input-output coefficients of the various labor groups dropped also. The hypothesis that technical change was labor-saving and capital-using, suggested as a possible explanation for the above observations, is investigated empirically.

Despite the vast expropriations of privately owned firms during the sixties, private establishments still exist in every branch of economic activity in Iraq. The existence of this dual ownership in most industries raises the interesting question of relative economic efficiency of the private versus the public sector. Chapter III presents analyses of the relative allocative and technical efficiency of private and government firms in the mineral, chemical and food processing industries in Iraq. Three concepts of economic efficiency (technical, allocative and policy efficiency) are analyzed and incorporated into a model of firm behavior. The main features of the model are that private and public firms within an industry do not have the same production functions, and profit maximization is not a maintained hypothesis. Statistical tests of the various economic efficiency hypotheses are derived and applied to the above industries. Finally, the results obtained in this chapter are linked to the analyses presented in Chapters I and II.

CHAPTER I

A DIVISIA INDEX ANALYSIS OF FACTOR PRODUCTIVITY

There are two distinct approaches to study the relative contributions of factor inputs and technical progress to economic growth. One is to estimate the rate of technical change and the marginal contributions of individual factors to output growth by using econometric methods. In the next essay a parametric method in an econometric model is developed and used to study the sources of economic growth.

The second approach, the one adopted in this chapter, is to use factor shares in the value of output as weights to combine the individual factor inputs and form an index of total factor input. Then, to denote the part of output growth which cannot be explained by increases in factor inputs as total factor productivity or technical change.

The difference between growth in measured output and the growth in measured inputs can be due to (1) factors other than those explicitly accounted for "technological change," (2) incorrect quantification of the variables explicitly listed, e.g., failure to account adequately for changes in the quality of labor, (3) the inaccuracy of the attribution that the reward a factor receives is an appropriate measure of its marginal product (as is the case of economies of scale, and perhaps monopoly power).

It is apparent that there are many possible causes of a residual through attention often focused on technological progress. Nevertheless, the residual approach to study the sources of growth does help to shed some light on the relative importance of factor input contribution and non-factor input contribution to growth.

I have used the Divisia index to measure the residual. This index can be devised from the assumptions of neoclassical theory. By assuming that a continuous twice differentiable production function exists, that it is homogeneous of degree one, and that all inputs are paid in proportion to their marginal revenue products, one can derive the index of the residual.

The Analytical Framework

The production function is written as

$$(1.1) \qquad Y(t) = F[x_1(t)\ldots, x_n(t), t]$$

where Y is output, x_i is the ith input and t is time. Taking the logarithm of the production function and differentiating with respect to time, gives

$$(1.2) \qquad \dot{Y}/Y = (\Sigma F_i \dot{x}_i)/F + F_t/F$$

where a dot over a symbol means the derivations with respect to time and $F_i = \frac{\partial F}{\partial x_i}$, $F_t = \frac{\partial F}{\partial t}$. F_t is the proportional rate of shift of the production function. It is taken to represent total factor productivity or technical progress. The assumptions made above allow us to set $\frac{F_i x_i}{F} = \alpha_i$, the shares of total output paid to the ith input.

Denoting the index of total factor productivity as R(t), we have the following equation defining the growth rate of this index

$$(1.3) \qquad \frac{\dot{R}}{R} = \dot{Y}/Y - \sum_{i=1}^{n} (\alpha_i \frac{\dot{x}_i}{x_i}).$$

The apparent shift of the function over time $\dot{R}/R$ is the growth rate of the Divisia index of the residual. We should note that the α_i may change through time along with x_i, y_i and the function F itself.

The conventional method of calculating the productivity index has been to apply a discrete approximation to equation (1.3) by assuming that factor shares are constant. As far as the experience of the industrialized countries is concerned, the factor shares in income have been stable, and hence most studies applied equation (1.3) with α_i as constant. In economies like Iraq when factor shares are changing over time, using the mean of the shares may yield biased results.

I thus prefer to use the following alternative discrete approximation to equation (1.2)

$$(1.4) \qquad \Delta Y_t = \sum_{i=1}^{n} w_{i,t-1}(x_{it} - x_{i,t-1}) + \Delta R_t$$

where w_i is the unit input cost. Equation (1.4) allocates the marginal increase in output each period among changes in input levels, using last period's unit cost as a weight, and the unexplained part is attributed to change in total factor productivity. Thus annual growth rates of the residual are first computed and then the annual average for a longer period is found and given. $\Delta R_t/R_t$ is computed using the following equation,

$$(1.5) \qquad \Delta R_t/R_{t-1} = \Delta Y_t/Y_{t-1} - \sum_{i=1}^{n} \left(\frac{w_{i,t-1} - x_{i,t-1}}{y_{t-1}}\right)\left(\frac{x_{it} - x_{i,t-1}}{x_{i,t-1}}\right)$$

or

$$(1.6) \qquad \dot{R}_t = \dot{Y}_t - \sum_{i=1}^{n} \alpha_{i,t-1}\dot{x}_{it}$$

Aggregation Bias

The use of aggregate data introduces possible bias in productivity analyses. In order to be able to add together different inputs, they must be homogeneous, namely each input must be perfectly substitutable for any other input: the marginal rate of substitution is constant and the units of measurement are chosen so that the marginal products of every unit are equal. Since these conditions are not satisfied in general, it is expected that the use of aggregated data in the Divisia index may cause a bias. It can be shown that if the prices of the inputs are equal or the growth rates of the inputs are equal, then aggregation does not bias the residual.[1] If there is a bias, disaggregation will reduce the residual when the input with the highest price grows the fastest. It will increase the residual when the input with the lowest price grows the fastest. The data used in this study provide classification of the labor input into six skill categories, so that a residual analysis with and without labor aggregation can be performed and compared.

Empirical Findings

The present section attempts to measure sources of growth of the industrial sector of Iraq. Being a socialist country, Iraq has a large government-owned industrial sector: the public share in total manufacturing grew from .25 in 1960 to about .75 in 1968, largely as a result of nationalization acts of 1964. The period under consideration is 1961-1967, and some results are obtained also for the longer period 1961-1975.

We focus our attention on the public sector but we make some comparison with the shrinking private sector.

The data for this study were collected from the annual industrial survey of Iraq, available since 1960, and from annual national accounts of the country. Consistent data for the labor force, disaggregated by six skill groups are available in each census (see Appendix for data descriptions).

Using equation (1.6) I constructed the index of total factor productivity. We begin by constructing indexes of total output, capital and labor services

[1] See Star (1974, p. 126).

for the public sector for the period 1961-1967. As an index of total output, I used gross of depreciation value added in constant prices. Labor input is measured by hours of work of the different skill groups. An index of energy use is used as an index for capital services in production (see Appendix for derivation and theoretical and empirical support for this index).

The average annual rate of growth of total output over this period is 17.92 percent. The average rate of growth of total input, constructed according to equation (1.6) is 16.12 percent. The average rate of growth of total factor productivity is 1.799 percent. The rate of gorwth of total input explains 89.9 percent of the growth in output of the public sector. The remainder is total factor productivity.

The average rate of growth of capital contribution is 12.34 percent accounting for 69 percent of output growth. The contribution of total labor to economic growth is 3.78, accounting for 21.1 percent of output growth. Among the labor inputs the group of skilled labor has the larger contribution to growth, 2.239 percent, while the contributions of unskilled and technical labor are .716 and .1763 percent respectively.

The application of equation (1.6) requires data for every year of the period analyzed. On the other hand, equation (1.3) is useful in a case when annual data is not available since it requires only data for the endpoints of the period we want to analyze. I used the mean value of the shares as weights to compose the Divisia index of inputs. This approximation has no estimation error if the actual mean income share is equal to the estimated shares. Using equation (1.3), the average rate of growth of total factor productivity is 2.31 percent, compared to 1.799 obtained by equation (1.6). This upward bias is a result of changes in income shares over time: the capital share rising while the labor share follows. Since capital has a much higher average growth rate, using the mean of the shares biases downward the measure of capital's contribution and impart an upward bias to the index of total factor productivity.

We turn next to the aggregation issue. We have eliminated errors of aggregation that arise in combining labor services into an index of total labor input by using different prices per man hour for each category in computing this index. If we assume that all labor categories are homogeneous, with equal price per man hour, the average rate of growth of total factor productivity is .716. This is to be compared with the 1.799 figure obtained when the Divisia index of total labor input is based on a weighted average of the rates of growth of different categories of labor, using relative shares in total labor compensation as weights. Thus aggregation of the labor inputs reduces the residual and impart a downward bias to the productivity index. This is a result of the fact that the inputs with the highest price, technical and managerial labor, grow the slowest, while skilled labor, which has a much lower wage rate, grows the fastest.

The results obtained above suggest that total factor productivity plays a moderate part in explaining the variations in the rate of output growth in the public sector in the period analyzed. The high average growth rates of output, labor and capital of the public sector, resulted from the expropriations of private firms by the government in 1964. In this year the value added produced by firms listed in the public sector was more than doubled and all big businesses were transferred to the hands of the government.

Thus the net rate of growth of the public sector output is much lower than the 17.92 percent reported before. In order to find the net rate growth of factor productivity we must also recognize that the relevant increments of labor and capital should not include resources transferred to the public sector through nationlization.

To clarify this issue we divided the period into two sub-periods: 1960-63 and 1964-67 and applied the Divisia index analysis. We thus eliminate the changes that occurred in 1964. The average annual rate of growth of output in the first period was 11.62 percent. The average rate of growth of capital and labor are 11.51 and 7.88 percent respectively. These growth rates, weighted by the input shares, account for an annual average rate of growth of output of 10.17 percent, leaving an unexplained residual of 1.446 percent per year. Thus total factor productivity explains 12.44 percent of total output growth.

In the years 1964-67 output growth was much lower, the annual growth rate was 6.83 percent. The annual average rate of growth of capital and labor are 8.07 and 4.6 respectively. The weighted contribution of inputs to output rate of growth is 6.93, leaving no unexplained residual. Thus total input growth explains all the change in ouput. Similar results are obtained for the private sector in this period. We thus conclude that there was no gain in factor productivity in the post-nationalization years.

This evidence indicates that compositional shifts account for a very large part of the gross productivity gain in the public sector in the decade of the 1960's.

To obtain the average net rate of growth of total factor productivity, we computed average growth rates of output and inputs for the public sector net of the resources transferred from the private sector in 1964. The net rate of growth of total factor productivity is 0.512 percent, lower than the 1.79 gross rate obtained before. By adding to the private sector the resources expropriated in 1964, we found that the net annual rate of growth of total factor productivity in this sector is 1.54, much higher than the gross value.

To summarize our findings, we conclude that a large part of the productivity change observed in the public sector in Iraq in the years 1961-67 can be explained by the nationalization of the most productive private firms. We do find net productivity growth in the public sector during the years 1960-1963 (average rate of growth of total factor productivity is 1.4 percent). We could not identify any productivity change, either in the public or in the private sector in the post-nationalization period.

The main factors explaining economic growth in Iraq are capital accumulation and labor growth. Total factor productivity growth plays a minor part in explaining output growth but it is much more important in the private sector than in the public sector (when a comparison between the net growth of this sector is made).

In order to have a better perspective of our results, it is useful to compare them with existing evidence on the developed and developing economies.

The literature on sources of growth reveals contrasting patterns of empirical evidence for the developed and developing countries. First, for a considerable time after the pioneering work of Abramovitz (1956) and Solow (1957), the findings had almost invariably been that total factor productivity constitutes by far the most important source of growth. Denison (1967) found that in all eight European developed countries[1] he studied, over 50 percent of output growth cannot be explained by increases in inputs even after allowance for quality change in labor inputs.

A somewhat different pattern of results has been found from the experience of the developing countries. The residual method as a growth accounting device has been applied to Latin American countries by Correa (1970) and Bruton (1967),

[1] The countries are: Belgium, Germany, Netherlands, Norway, Denmark, France, Italy and United Kingdom.

to the Philippines by Williamson (1969) and to Israel by Gaathon (1961). In these studies, it is found that the contribution of factor inputs to growth has been much more important than those of total factor productivity. For Correa's study of nine Latin American countries[1] during the period 1950-62, an average of 34 percent of output growth is explained by total factor productivity. Bruton's study of five Latin American countries during 1960-64 shows an even lower percentage of 28. For Asian economies, it is 39 percent for the Philippines in 1955-70, 31 percent for Israel in 1950-65, and 24 percent for India in 1950-60 (Psacharopolous, 1969).

Using Denison's findings, the average for the nine Western countries during the period 1950-1962 is 64 percent. Thus our results are in line with the findings in the literature for the developing countries. The rate of growth of total factor productivity in Iraq in the years before nationalization is among the highest, similar to that of Chile, Ecuador, Peru and Venezuela, but since output growth rate in Iraq is much higher, its relative contribution is at the bottom of the list.

The results suggest that the contribution of capital to growth is greater than that of labor. This is not surprising since Iraq is not a relatively labor-abundant economy and economic resources for capital formation are available from oil revenues and foreign Arab funds. No similar studies for other rich oil Middle Eastern countries are available at the moment for comparison with the results obtained for Iraq.

The main assumptions behind the Divisia index analyses are the homogeneity of degree one assumption (constant returns to scale), constant neutral rate of technical change, and payments to factors of production according to their

---

[1]The countries are: Argentina, Brazil, Chile, Colombia, Ecuador, Honduras, Mexico, Peru and Venezuela.

marginal productivities. In the next chapter I develop a parametric framework to study factor productivity in which the above assumptions are relaxed and the sensitivity of the results to them is assessed. The model is applied to the 1961-67 Iraqi data.

CHAPTER II

TOTAL FACTOR PRODUCTIVITY, NON-NEUTRAL TECHNICAL CHANGE AND ECONOMIC GROWTH: A PARAMETRIC STUDY OF THE INDUSTRIAL SECTOR OF IRAQ

Employment problems in less developed countries (LDC's) have received much attention in the development literature. The low level of labor absorption in the industrial sector along its growth path and the existence of large scale unemployment in many developing economies centered much of the attention on the sources and causes of economic growth and the determinants of the technology used in LDC's. Technical change, capital accumulation and investment in education are considered to be the most important factors affecting economic growth, but their effects have not been quantified for many LDC's.

In this chapter we analyze the manufacturing sector of a socialist developing economy, Iraq, and attempt to measure the contributions of technological progress and primary factors of production to economic growth.

The observed low rates of employment generation may suggest that the growth of efficiency of conventional inputs may be non-neutral in the sense that the marginal productivities of those inputs do not increase at the same rate through time. We thus attempt to give an answer to the question of whether there have been any biases in the direction of technical change and to measure such biases and their implications for employment problems.

Productivity is often measured as a ratio of output to inputs. The most important indices are the partial productivity indices (of labor and capital) and the total productivity index. The former indices are simply the average products of labor or capital, while total factor productivity, often referred to as the "residual," or index of technical progress, is defined as output per unit of labor and capital combined.[1]

Productivity indices are deduced from explicitly defined production functions. Thus accurate specification of the form and estimation of the parameters of the production function are crucial to measurement of these indices. Most "residual methods" are based on the Cobb-Douglas or constant elasticity of substitution production function, with homogeneity or constant returns to scale as a maintained hypothesis and autonomous and neutral technological change postulated. Further, assuming that factors are paid in proportion to their marginal productivity, the observed average income shares of capital and labor are used in order to disentangle the growth of productivity or technical progress over time, from the growth of factors of production.

Intuitively one feels that there are many cases in which such simplifications might give biased results. The use of such expressions as "non-competitive equilibrium" and "structural disequilibrium" when talking of developing economies has become rather common. These points require even more attention when attempting to study growth of the public production sector in a socialist country.

Since in Iraq the rate of growth of capital has been considerably higher than that of labor, productivity analyses will be sensitive to the assumption regarding the distribution of income between labor and capital. The assumption of marginal productivity equal opportunity cost of capital may be far from reality in the public sector, and we thus avoid using it.

The purpose of this chapter is to develop a parametric approach to the analyses of total and specific factor productivity and to apply it to the public

---

[1]In Chapter I, a version of the "residual" had been used to analyze total factor productivity in Iraq.

manufacturing sector of Iraq. The contribution of a parametric approach is that it does not rely on the assumption of constant returns to scale; it allows the returns to scale to be non-homothetic, homothetic, or homogenous. Non-neutral technical change is modeled, estimated and linked to the conventional average input specific productivity indices. Using duality theory the parametric approach is derived in a restriced profit function, dual to the production function, which allows for capital services not to be paid the value of marginal product ("structural disequilibrium"). The parametric results are compared with results of residual analyses derived for the dual profit model.

An additional issue taken up in this chapter is the interaction in production among various groups of labor inputs of different skills, and among human and physical capital. The ease of substituting factor inputs in production has been considered as a factor affecting total factor productivity. The concept of an educational bottleneck as a barrier to economic growth in poor countries is based on the assumption of low elasticity of substitution among labor inputs. In a developing economy such as Iraq, where human capital is relatively scarce, high values for the above elasticities could ease the short run constraint on growth imposed by the lack of educated labor.

Measurement of the elasticities of substitution gained more importance from the surge of interest in educational planning adopted by many developing countries once the contribution of education to economic growth has been learned. The two main approaches to educational planning, the rate of return analyses and the manpower requirement approach, both make restrictive assumptions regarding the elasticities of substitution among labor inputs. The first approach assumes constant relative wage rates, implying an infinite elasticity of substitution, while in the second approach the elasticity of substitution among labor factors (and between them and other factors) is taken to be zero; the labor requirements of the economy may be deduced from the projected pattern of output, without reference to the relative cost of labor. Since Iraq, as many other developing economies, has adopted the Leontief input-output analyses as the basis for the manpower requirements approach to educational planning, we assess the basic assumptions of this approach by estimating a set of elasticities of substitution derived from the dual profit function. Since our model allows for complementarity among factors of production, it is of interest to compare our results to other studies that measured the ease of substitution among labor inputs (Bowles [1970], Dougherty [1972], Fallon and Layard [1975]).

In what follows, the next section outlines the theoretical framework, and estimation issues are discussed. We then present and analyze the empirical results, followed by some concluding remarks.

Theoretical Foundations

Production theory and functional forms for the production function serve as the theoretical foundations for productivity analyses.

It is assumed that there exists an aggregate production function, F, expressing the maximum attainable output (V), from a flow services (X) and fixed inputs (K). The production function F, which is assumed to be differentiable of the required order,[1] is specified as:

$$(2.1) \qquad V = F(X, K, t) = F(N, U, S, T, K, t)$$

where N is services of administrative workers, while U, S, and T are production labor groups classified by skill: U is unskilled labor, S is skilled labor and T is technical labor, the most human capital intensive group of workers (more detailed

[1]The production function is continuously twice differentiable, strictly monotone, and strictly quasi-concave.

descriptions of these variables and the data are given in the Appendix). K represents the flow services of capital while t is a technology index introduced to represent technological effects on the production function.

The role of capital accumulation as a major source of economic growth has been well quantified in empirical studies accounting for the growth of output in many countries. The contribution of capital is usually derived by assuming that capital is paid in proportion to its marginal revenue product. Imposing this behavioral assumption may be far from reality in a socialist developing country in which capital accumulation is governed by a periodical development plan which does not necessarily use strict economic efficiency criteria as its guidelines. Assuming that the distribution of capital in the economy is given at each moment of time without imposing an optimality condition, seems an appropriate alternative.

Rather than estimate the production function directly, it is more adequate to have a model that incorporates explicitly the fixity of capital and allows its marginal productivity to be different from its opportunity cost. It is thus assumed that a public firm manager is trying to minimize the variable cost of production utilizing the stock of capital installed in the plant. If the distribution of capital in the economy is optimal, the estimated marginal productivity of capital should be treated as its true opportunity cost.

I choose to utilize a normalized restricted profit function from which the properties of the underlying production function can be derived using duality theory. Normalized restricted profit is defined as

$$V(X, K, t) - \sum_{i=1}^{4} W_i X_i$$

where V is the value of output deflated by its price and W_i is the wage rate of the ith labor group divided by the price of output. The manager facing given wages chooses quantities of variable inputs that maximize normalized restricted profit. Thus

$$\pi = F(X^*, K, t) - \sum_{i=1}^{4} W_i X_i^*$$
$$= \pi(W, K, t)$$

where X_i^* are the optimal amounts of labor, and π is the maximum restricted profit, deflated by the price of output, and W is the vector of real wages.

For purposes of empirical implementation, it is necessary to specify an explicit functional form for π. Since our aim is to develop and implement a parametric approach to the measurement of total factor productivity, we need a form that relaxes the assumptions made in the traditional residual methods. A number of flexible functional forms of the noramlized restricted profit function could be estimated (see Lau [1976] and Diewert [1973]). We choose to use the transcendental logarithm (translog) form (see Christensen, Jorgensen and Lau [1973] and Lau [1976]), which is flexible enough to identify simultaneously the return to scale form of the dual production function (non-homothetic, homothetic, homogenous), total factor productivity, non-neutral patterns of technical change and substitution elasticities among factors of production.

A translog normalized restricted profit function has the following form:

$$(2.2) \qquad \ln \pi = \alpha_0 + \sum_{i=1}^{4} \alpha_i \ln W_i + \frac{1}{2} \sum_{i}^{4} \sum_{j}^{4} \gamma_{ij} \ln W_i \ln W_j + \sum_{i=1}^{4} \beta_{ij} \ln W_i \ln K + \beta_K \ln K + \frac{1}{2} \beta_{KK} (\ln K)^2 + \sum_{i=1}^{4} \delta_{it} \ln W_i t + \delta_t t + \frac{1}{2} \delta_{tt} t^2 + \delta_{K_t} \ln Kt$$

It is obtained by a Taylor logarithmic expansion up to the second order terms of the normalized restricted profit π.

The form of the dual production function can be derived from the restricted profit function using duality theory. By Hoteling's lemma

$$(2.3)\qquad V^* = \pi^* - \Sigma W_i \frac{\partial \pi}{\partial W_i}$$

$$(2.4)\qquad X_i^* = -\frac{\partial \pi}{\partial W_i}$$

where V^* and X_i^* are the profit maximizing supply of output and demand of input i respectively.

The production function F is homothetic in X and K (under certain regularity conditions (see Lau [1976]) if and only if

$$(2.5)\qquad \sum_{i=1}^{4} \frac{\partial F}{\partial X_i} X_i + \frac{\partial F}{\partial K} K = f[F(X, K)]$$

where f is an arbitrary, finite, non-negative function of a single variable with $f(0) = 0$. Using the relations given in equations (2.3) and (2.4), it can be shown that the production function F is homothetic in X and K if and only if the normalize profit function satisfies equation (2.6):

$$(2.6)\qquad -\Sigma W_i \frac{\partial \pi}{\partial W_i} + \frac{\partial \pi}{\partial K} K = f(\pi - \sum_{i=1}^{4} W_i \frac{\partial \pi}{\partial W_i})$$

Differentiating (2.6) with respect to W_i and K yields the following necessary and sufficient restrictions for the translog function to satisfy equation (2.6):

$$(2.7a)\qquad \lambda \sum_{i=1}^{4} \gamma_{ij} + \beta_{jK} = \phi\alpha_j \qquad i, j = N, U, S, T$$

$$(2.7b)\qquad \lambda \sum_{i=1}^{4} \beta_{iK} + \beta_{KK} = \phi\beta_K$$

where

$$\phi = f'(1 - \sum_{i=1}^{4} \frac{\partial \ln \pi}{\partial \ln W_i} - \frac{f}{\pi}) \text{ and } \lambda = f' - 1$$

and f' is assumed constant at the point of approximation.[1]

The homothetic production function F is homogenous if and only if equation (2.8) holds

$$(2.8) \qquad f[F(X, K)] = kF(X, K)$$

which is the familiar Euler theorem, and a specialization of equation (2.5). In terms of the dual profit structure, the production function F is homogeneous of degree k if and only if equation (2.6) and the following equation are satisfied,

$$(2.9) \qquad f(\pi - \sum_{i=1}^{4} W_i \frac{\partial \pi}{\partial W_i} = k(\pi - \sum_{i=1}^{4} W_i \frac{\partial \pi}{\partial W_i}$$

When the restricted profit function satisfies equations (2.6) and (2.9), f is equal to k, the degree of return to scale (which is now constant everywhere) and $\phi = 0$. Thus, homogeneity of F can be tested by adding the restriction $\phi = 0$ to those of homotheticity given by (2.7a) and (2.7b).

We now turn to the analyses of technical change and the measurement of total factor productivity. Technical change is defined as movement in the production function, namely a change in output that is not a result of changes in the level of inputs. In a production function technical change is measured by $\frac{\partial F}{\partial t}$. In the dual profit structure the effect of time is captured by $\frac{\partial \pi}{\partial t}$. By duality $\frac{\partial F}{\partial t} = \frac{\partial \pi}{\partial t}$ at the profit maximum. The normalized restricted translog profit function yields the following dual rate of total factor productivity

$$(2.10) \qquad \frac{\partial \ln \pi}{\partial t} = \delta_t + \delta_{tt} t + \sum_{i=1}^{4} \delta_{it} \ln W_i + \delta_{Kt} \ln K$$

where all inputs are held constant. Hence for given W_i's and K's normalized profit increase with time. The gain in restricted profits can be described as a result of a

[1]The point of approximation is the geometric mean of the sample.

reduction in the quantity of inputs required to produce a given amount of output. The dual rate of total factor productivity given by (2.10) reflects the reduction in input requirements indirectly through cost reduction captured by the effect of variable input prices and directly through the changes in quantity of fixed inputs required in production.

The translog specification is flexible enough to allow for different neutral and non-neutral patterns of technical change. The most common neutral patterns are the Hicks and Harrod technical changes. The restricted profit function is Hicks neutral if the ratio of the derived demand of any two variable inputs (or the ratio of a derived demand and the marginal productivity of a fixed input) is independent of technical change. The restricted profit function will be Hicks neutral if

$$\delta_{it} = 0 \quad i = N, U, S, T \tag{2.11a}$$

$$\delta_{iK} = 0 \tag{2.11b}$$

If the production function is homothetic, Hicksian neutrality of the restricted profit function implies Hicksian neutrality of the production function (Lau [1976a]. If the production function is not homothetic, Hicksian neutrality of the restricted profit function implies that technical change is "output augmenting" and "factor saving" at equal rates.

The normalized profit function is Harrod neutral if the ratio of the demand for labor to the dual rate of total factor productivity is independent of the quantity of capital. The restricted profit function will be Harrod neutral if

$$\beta_{iK} = 0 \quad i = N, U, S, T \tag{2.12a}$$

$$\beta_{tK} = 0 \tag{2.12b}$$

A technical change process is factor i saving if it causes its expenditure profit ratio to fall, holding constant output, prices and capital. In the dual profit model technical change is variable input saving if $\frac{\partial \ln \pi}{\partial \ln W \partial t} > 0$. For the translog specification this implies that technical change is input i-saving, i-neutral or i-using according to whether δ_{it} is less than, equal to, or greater than zero, respectively.

To study substitution possibilities among factors of production in the dual profit framework when capital is assumed a fixed factor, we make use of a modified Allen partial elasticity of substitution defined as,

$$\text{(2.13a)} \qquad \sigma_{ii} = \frac{E_{ii}}{S_i} = \frac{-S_i^2 - S_i - \gamma_{ii}}{S_i^2}$$

$$\text{(2.13b)} \qquad \sigma_{ij} = \frac{E_{ij}}{S_j} = \frac{-S_i S_j - \gamma_{ij}}{S_i S_j}$$

where E_{ii} and E_{ij} are the own and cross price elasticities, derived under the assumption that quantity rather than the price of the fixed input is held constant, and the price rather than the quantity of output is held constant.

The profit model permits us also to examine the substitution and complementarity relationships between the variable labor inputs and the fixed capital input. Since the shadow price of capital which is equal to its marginal productivity is given as

$$\frac{\partial \pi}{\partial K} = \frac{\pi}{K}(\beta_K + \beta_{KK} + \sum_{i=1}^{4} \beta_{iK} \ln W_i + \delta_{KL} t)$$

we cannot vary it independently. We thus make use of the following definition: two inputs are complements if increasing the supply of one increases the marginal product of the other (increases its optimal amount) and substitutes if increasing the supply decreases the other's marginal product (while output is held constant).

Estimation

Demand functions for the variable inputs are obtained by logarithmic differentiation of the normalized restricted profit function

$$\text{(2.14)} \qquad \frac{\partial \ln \pi}{\partial \ln W_i} = \frac{\partial \pi}{\partial W_i} \frac{W_i}{\pi} = \alpha_i + \sum_{j=1}^{4} \gamma_{ij} \ln W_i + \beta_{iK} \ln K + \delta_{it} t$$

By Hoteling's lemma $\frac{\partial \pi}{\partial W_i} = -X_i^*$ where X_i^* is the cost-minimizing quantity of input i. Substituting $-X_i^*$ in (2.13) to get

$$\frac{\partial \ln \pi}{\partial \ln W_i} = -\frac{X_i^* W_i}{\pi} = -S_i = \alpha_i + \Sigma \alpha_{ij} \ln W_j + \beta_{iK} \ln K + \delta_{it} t$$

where S_i is the ratio of the expenditure on input i and profit.

The set of equations to be estimated consists of the restricted profit equation (2.2) and the factor demand equations (2.13). An additive disturbance term is appended to each equation to allow for random errors in cost-maximizing behavior.[1]

The data used in this study are obtained by pooling time series (1961-1967) and cross section (13 regions of Iraq) observations. Since there might be differences in product mix and production efficiency between the regions, this fact has to be taken into consideration in the stochastic specification. We use a co-variance estimation procedure in its dummy variable form. We assume that the error term u_i of each derived demand and v, the profit function disturbance term are each

[1]An alternative stochastic specification would be to assume that the production function is stochastic and to derive the dual profit function directly. The cost minimizing errors should also affect the profit function, so that the profit function involves two error terms, the production function error and the cost minimization error. This modeling is very complicated for flexible forms with second order terms (see Chapter III for such stochastic modeling with a Cobb-Douglas production function).

composed of two stochastic components: a region-specific component and an overall component. The region-specific component is assumed constant over time and we add it to the intercept of each equation so that each region has a different intercept in each equation. Denoting ε_i as the non-region component, the vector of disturbance terms $(\varepsilon_\pi, \varepsilon_U, \varepsilon_S, \varepsilon_T, \varepsilon_N)$ is assumed to be independently and identically normally distributed with mean zero and non-singular covariance matrix Ω .

Because cross-equation constraints are imposed in performing tests of hypotheses, the equations are estimated jointly. The estimates will be consistent since it is assumed that all explanatory variables, wages and capital services are exogenous. The results reported in the next section were computed using the Wymer Full Information Maximum Likelihood (FIML) Resimul program.

To test whether or not the loss of fit from imposing restrictions is significant, the model is estimated with and without the restrictions imposed. Since we obtained maximum likelihood estimates, the results may be compared by using the likelihood ratio test. Denoting the determinants of the unrestricted and restricted matrix of the disturbance covariance matrix by $|\hat{\Omega}_R|$ and $|\hat{\Omega}_U|$ respectively, we can write the likelihood ratio as $\lambda = (|\hat{\Omega}_R|/|\hat{\Omega}_U|)^{-N/2}$ where N is the number of observations. The statistic $-2 \ln \lambda$ computed to test all restrictions, is distributed asymptotically as chi-squared with degrees of freedom equal to the number of independent restrictions being imposed.

A normalized restricted profit function is well behaved only if it is strictly decreasing and convex in the normalized prices and strictly increasing in the fixed input. The translog form is an approximation to the true profit function and it possesses non-economic regions; therefore the above properties have to be verified at each observation point.

The condition that the restricted profit function be strictly decreasing in normalized prices is checked by examining the fitted ratios for positivity. The

TABLE 1

PROFIT FUNCTION PARAMETER ESTIMATES
(t-ratios in parentheses)

Parameter	NHT-H	NHT-Hicks-N	NHT-Harrod-N	HOMT	HOMG	Parameter	NHT-H	NHT-Hicks-N	NHT-Harrod-N	HOMT	HOMG
α_U	-.3747	-.3953	-.0336	-.5358	-.8185	β_K	.5552	-.1858	-.3428	4.3080	.7616
	(3.04)	(2.67)	(.32)	(4.76)	(4.89)		(1.52)	(0.53)	(.89)	(8.06)	(5.65)
α_S	-2.744	-2.6103	.2469	-3.109	-2.037	β_{KK}	.1454	.2379	.1345	-.2960	.0082
	(6.04)	(4.98)	(.49)	(5.70)	(3.27)		(3.62)	(5.76)	(3.07)	(5.02)	(2.11)
α_T	-.1363	-.1625	.0590	-.0484	-.1144	β_{UK}	.0328	.0349	--	.0375	.0202
	(1.57)	(2.03)	(.79)	(.91)	(1.33)		(6.33)	(6.66)		(7.37)	(3.88)
α_N	-1.4165	-1.5042	.1489	-1.1125	-1.517	β_{SK}	.2105	.2183	--	.2230	.0437
	(8.04)	(8.06)	(.67)	(5.47)	(5.90)		(9.78)	(10.1)		(9.35)	(2.40)
γ_{UU}	.0259	.0341	.0409	.0964	-.0345	β_{TK}	.0071	.0082	--	.0062	.0011
	(.86)	(1.42)	(1.72)	(4.06)	(1.37)		(2.16)	(2.5)		(1.91)	(.49)
γ_{SS}	.0677	.1654	.2959	.1106	-.1736	β_{NK}	.0956	.0982	--	.0822	.0374
	(.47)	(1.09)	(1.71)	(.72)	(1.13)		(12.63)	(12.9)		(10.41)	(4.33)
γ_{TT}	.0055	.0068	-.0004	.000	-.0009	δ_t	-.0138	-.1589	.0683	.6167	-.1364
	(.47)	(.59)	(.04)	(.00)	(.08)		(1.12)	(1.98)	(.74)	(3.48)	(.95)
γ_{NN}	-.0182	-.0457	.0754	.0719	-.1577	δ_{tt}	.0182	.0389	.0245	-.1068	.0176
	(.43)	(.32)	(.10)	(1.09)	(3.40)		(2.17)	(2.31)	(1.34)	(3.63)	(.96)
γ_{US}	.0001	-.0121	-.0112	-.1477	-.1205	δ_{Ut}	.0060	--	.0088	.0060	.0098
	(.00)	(.28)	(.26)	(3.51)	(2.70)		(2.82)		(3.38)	(3.07)	(4.06)
γ_{UT}	.0018	.0016	.0061	-.0111	-.0081	δ_{St}	.0292	--	.0420	.0201	.0507
	(.17)	(.17)	(.58)	(.79)	(.75)		(3.33)		(3.28)	(2.31)	(4.17)
γ_{UA}	-.0102	.007	.0027	.0280	-.0889	δ_{Tt}	.0058	--	.0059	.0053	.0064
	(.43)	(.32)	(.10)	(1.09)	(3.40)		(4.31)		(4.25)	(4.08)	(4.89)
γ_{ST}	-.0182	-.024	.0229	.0319	-.0177	δ_{At}	.0082	--	.0141	.0096	.0175
	(.65)	(.88)	(.83)	(.76)	(.70)		(2.64)		(2.62)	(3.16)	(3.79)
γ_{SA}	-.0945	-.1358	.0694	-.1289	-.2318	δ_{Kt}	.0101	--	--	-.0086	.0362
	(1.78)	(2.3)	(.90)	(1.82)	(3.35)		(.99)			(.50)	(3.16)
γ_{TA}	.0182	..0108	.0265	.0111	.0122	α_0	-7.666	-4.498	4.071	-22.67	-3.849
	(1.22)	(.73)	(1.56)	(.60)	(.83)		(3.83)	(2.4)	(2.32)	(9.39)	(2.05)

condition that the restricted profit function be strictly increasing in the fixed input is checked by computing its marginal productivity

$$\frac{\partial \pi}{\partial K} = \frac{\pi}{K}(\beta_K + \beta_{KK} + \sum_{i=1}^{4} \beta_{iK} \ln W_i + \delta_{Kt} t)$$

for each observation.

Convexity in normalized prices requires the Hessian of the restricted profit function to be positive definite for each observation. This will be true if and only if all the eigen values are positive, a test to be carried out for all observations.

Empirical Results

In this section we report results of estimating the model under three different returns to scale specifications for the production function: non-homothetic (NHT), homothetic (HOMT) and homogeneous (HOMG). Each of these specifications is analyzed with three forms of technical change: non-neutral (NN), Hicks neutral (HN) and Harrod neutral (HARN). In Table 1 we give the parameter estimates and their asymptotic standard errors obtained from the inverse of the information matrix. Also in each table we give the log likelihood values which are used subsequently for hypothesis testing.

The condition that the restricted profit function be decreasing in the prices of variable inputs implies that the fitted expenditure ratios should be positive. All of the nine models estimated performed very well in that all fitted ratios (but three in some of the models) are positive.

The marginal productivity of the fixed inputs is positive for all models at all observation points, satisfying the second condition for a well behaved restricted profit function.

Convexity of the restricted profit function is checked by determining whether the eigen values of the estimated Hessian matrices are positive. Negative values were found for very few observations, except for the rejected homogenous model, for which there were about 15 negative eigen values. Although this procedure does not constitute a statistical test of convexity, the numerical convexity check supports somewhat the assumption of variable cost minimization in the public sector.

One set of parameter estimates not reported in Table 1 is that for the regional dummy variables. Strong regional efficiency differences are revealed by the very significant values of most of the region dummies in all the models estimate In addition to efficiency and product mix differences among the regions, the dummy variables may capture also systematic deviations from the country average index of output price which we used to deflate output and wages.

The results of statistical tests of the returns to scale and technologica change specifications are summarized in Table 2. The homotheticity and homogeneity

TABLE 2

TESTS OF HYPOTHESES

	Nbr. of Index Restrictions	χ^2 Critical Value .01	.025	Value of χ^2 Test Statistic
NHT Hicks Neutral	5	13.28	11.14	22.61
NHT Harrod Neutral	5	13.28	11.14	110.60
HOMT	33	50.89	46.98	103.1
HOMT Hicks Neutral	5	16.81	14.45	29.3
HOMT Harrod Neutral	5	16.81	14.45	112.6
HOMG	34	50.89	46.98	131.4
HOMG Hicks Neutral	5	16.81	14.45	21.4
HOMG Harrod Neutral	5	16.81	14.45	110.3

hypotheses are rejected regardless of the form of technical change. Furthermore, Hicks and Harrod neutral technical change are both rejected irrespective of the returns to scale specified.

We found strong statistical evidence supporting the hypothesis that technical change is not neutral. In all the non-neutral models, technical change is labor-saving and capital-using. The labor non-neutrality parameters δ_{it} are all positive with high t-statistics, and their values are not sensitive to the homotheticity and homogeneity specification.

An indicative index for the biases is given by the following elasticity:[1]

$$\eta_{X^*_{it}} = \frac{\partial \ln X^*_i}{\partial t} = -\delta_{it}/S_i$$

which relates the rate of change of the optimal amount of a factor to be used in production as a result of the passage of time. It is derived holding constant wages, capital and profit. The rates for the three models are summarized in Table 3. These rates show a very strong labor-saving bias, similar for the unskilled, skilled and administrative groups, but twice as large for the technical labor group. It is reasonable to assume that the price of labor is to a great extent governed by wage rates in other sectors of the economy, and exogenous to the manufacturing sector to a substantial extent because of its relative small size. The price of labor increased throughout the period 1961-1967, with the exception of the real wages of technical labor. Real wages grew at an annual average rate of 2.71 percent for unskilled workers, 0.33 percent for skilled workers, 1.71 percent for administrative employees, and fell at a rate of 2.04 percent for technical labor.

---

[1]The actual effect of a technical change on X^*_i is given by $\frac{\partial \ln X^*_i}{\partial t} = -[\delta_{ti}/S_i + \frac{\partial \ln \pi}{\partial t}]$. It is composed of two components, a neutral effect given by $\frac{\partial \ln \pi}{\partial t}$ and a specific effect given by δ_{ti}/S_i. By holding constant profit, we mean just looking at the specific factor effect.

TABLE 3

ELASTICITIES OF OPTIMAL LABOR DEMAND
WITH RESPECT TO TIME

	η_{Ut}	η_{St}	η_{Tt}	η_{Nt}
Non-Homothetic	-.0772 (.027)	-.0691 (.0043)	-.1467 (.010)	-.0554 (.002)
Homothetic	-.0772 (.025)	-.0476 (.0033)	-.1346 (.0190)	-.0647 (.0056)
Homogenous	-.1256 (.020)	-.1200 (.0134)	-.1625 (.0234)	-.1180 (.0094)

The behavior of the labor bias is consistent with an induced innovation hypothesis except for the pattern of technical labor-saving, since it is associated with an input whose real cost went down over the sample period.

This significant labor-saving pattern can explain a large part of the observed reduction in the share of labor in value added, which dropped from 0.387 in 1961 to 0.267 in 1967, i.e., a drop of 41.6 percent in a period of just seven years.

The interpretation of these bias rates can be augmented by linking them to the conventional partial productivity indices. Defining average productivity of a factor as V/X, we derive the elasticity of the ith factor average productivity with respect to technical change as

$$\frac{\partial \ln(V/X_i)}{\partial t} = \frac{\partial \ln V}{\partial t} - \frac{\partial \ln X_i}{\partial t} = \frac{\partial \ln \pi}{\partial t} + \delta_{ti}/S_i$$

where capital and wages are held constant. Technical change raises average productivity of all factors at an equal rate given by $\frac{\partial \ln \pi}{\partial t}$ and has an additional effect specific to each factor, given by δ_{ti}/S_i, which is just the negative of the bias rate $\eta_{X^*_{it}}$ derived above. The higher the saving bias, the larger the increase in average productivity of each factor.

Examining the rate of change of actual average productivity, we found that the highest rate is that of technical labor, a rise of 67.8 percent versus 41.5 and 14.8 percent for unskilled and skilled labor respectively. This is just in line with our parametric framework results.

Since the capital service variable is introduced as an exogenous variable in our model, the effect of technical change cannot be formulated as the effect of time on the optimal amount of capital. Nevertheless, non-neutral effects on capital may be studied through examining the effects of time on its endogenous marginal productivity given by

$$(2.15) \qquad \frac{\partial(\partial\pi/\partial K)}{\partial t} = \frac{\partial \ln \pi}{\partial t}\,\frac{\partial \pi}{\partial K} + \delta_{Kt}\,\frac{\pi}{K}$$

where capital and wages are held constant. The first part of (2.15) is the neutral effect component on marginal productivity, while $\delta_{Kt}\,\frac{\pi}{K}$ is the non-neutral effect of time on capital productivity. If δ_{Kt} is positive, capital's marginal productivity rises by more than the average of all factors, changes the marginal rate of substitution between capital and other inputs, and induces more intensive use of capital. The sign of δ_{Kt} is used as a test for the direction of the bias in technical change.

In the non-homothetic and homothetic models δ_{Kt} is not significantly different from zero, indicating capital-neutral change, but since strong evidence for labor-saving was found, technical change was capital-using in relative terms. For the homogenous model δ_{Kt} is positive with low standard error, evidence for absolute and relative capital using technical change.

In Chapter I we found that the government of Iraq nationalized in 1964 the most productive firms of the private sector. If these firms were more capital intensive than the average public firm, it may be reflected in the form of labor-saving technical change. In order to find out whether the labor biases in technical change that we estimated are real and not merely a reflection of compositional shifts, we divided the period into two sub-periods: 1961-63 and 1964-67, and analyzed each period separately. We thus eliminate the changes that occurred in 1964. Table 4 summarizes the point estimates of the labor-saving parameters.

TABLE 4

LABOR SAVING PARAMETER ESTIMATES
(asymptotic t values in parentheses)

Parameter	1961-63	1964-67	1961-67
δ_{Ut}	.00612 (2.121)	.00484 (1.842)	.0060 (2.82)
δ_{St}	.0732 (2.687)	.00598 (1.123)	.0292 (3.332)
δ_{Tt}	.0197 (2.093)	.0025 (1.923)	.0058 (4.311)
δ_{At}	.0096 (1.928)	.0028 (.4213)	.0082 (2.641)

These estimates indicate that expropriations of private firms cannot account for the strong labor biases we found. The sign of the δ_{ti} estimates are the same for the sub-periods as for the period as a whole though the values and precision of the estimates vary somewhat. Thus technological change was labor biased before and after the expropriations in 1964.

The strong labor biased technical change found in Iraq has important implications for the employment problem in LDC's. In a number of countries in Latin America, Africa and Asia, despite significant investments in manufacturing, employment in this sector grew less rapidly than population, and in some cases even declined in absolute terms. The high biased rates estimated above can explain partly the poor contribution of the industrial sector to employment growth over the last two decades in many developing economies.

Total Factor Productivity

We now proceed to use the dual rate of total factor productivity $\frac{\partial \pi}{\partial t}$ derived in Section II to asses the contribution of technological change to output growth.

To analyze the sensitivity of productivity measurement to the specification of returns to scale and neutral technical change, Table 5 summarizes the estimated rate of growth of total productivity under the various hypotheses.

TABLE 5

ESTIMATED GROWTH RATES OF TOTAL FACTOR PRODUCTIVITY
(asymptotic standard errors in parentheses)

	NHOT	HOMT	HOMG
Non-Neutral	.01297 (.006)	.00941 (.003)	.02056 (.005)
Hicks Neutral	.00117 (.008)	.0008 (.010)	.00527 (.008)
Harrod Neutral	.00398 (.010)	.0012 (.008)	.0072 (.009)

Note: The values in the table are the elasticities $\partial \ell n\ \pi/\partial t$. To obtain percentage growth rates, they should be multiplied by one-hundred.

Table 5 shows that the measurement of total factor productivity is sensitive to the homotheticity, homogeneity and neutrality assumptions (all of them rejected statistically for our sample). Productivity, which grows at a rate of 1.297 percent a year in the non-homothetic model, drops to a growth rate of .941 percent under the homotheticity hypothesis and jumps to 2.056 percent when homogeneity is imposed. Since total productivity gain, as defined below, includes also gains from economies or diseconomies that arise due to changes in the scale of operation of the economy, it is not surprising to find how very sensitive $\frac{\partial\pi}{\partial t}$ is to the various scale assumptions.

Imposing homotheticity on the returns to scale yields $\lambda = -.08$ at the point of approximation, which implies that production is characterized by diseconomies of scale at that point. Thus the rejected homothetic model which implies that returns to scale are evenly distributed among all factors of production tends to depress the measurement of total factor productivity because of the rejected diseconomies of scale it imposes at the geometric mean of the sample.

Constraining the returns to scale parameter k to be constant everywhere has an opposite effect in our data. Under the homogeneity hypothesis we find substantial economies of scale that are reflected in productivity gain that grows at an annual rate of 2.056 percent. An estimate of λ, the returns to scale parameter, is equal to .08032 with a standard error equal to .0201. Therefore, the degree of returns to scale calculated as $\lambda + 1$ is equal to 1.0803, significantly greater than unity. The 95 percent confidence interval is 1.0602 - 1.1004.

It is interesting to observe that both the Hicks and Harrod neutrality restrictions tend to reduce substantially the rate of total factor productivity regardless of the form of returns to scale. Imposing the assumption that new techniques are such that they lead to equal saving in all inputs is decisively rejected by our data.

It is of interest to see how the results of the "residual" growth accounting method compares with the parametric results. In Chapter I we found that the average gross rate of growth of total factor productivity is 1.799 percent. This rate derived while using aggregate manufacturing sector data for the period 1961-1967, under the assumption of constant returns to scale, is much higher than the rate obtained parametrically from the non-homothetic model, but close to the rate obtained under the homogeneity assumption. This result indicates that productivity analyses are sensitive to the assumptions made regarding returns to scale and the form of technical change.

The low rate of growth of total factor productivity relative to the rate of growth of output suggest again, as found in Chapter I, that growth of primary inputs is the major cause of economic growth in Iraq.

Substitution and Complementarity Estimates

Another factor considered to have effects on total factor productivity is the ease of changing factors of production in the course of the production process. We do not derive direct relationships between these two endogenous parameters, but rather we focus our attention on the nature of substitution among the different production labor groups, and the interaction of skill and physical capital in production. The partial elasticities of substitution among production workers are

$$\sigma_{US} = -.9966 \qquad \sigma_{UT} = -1.575 \qquad \sigma_{ST} = .0924$$

The unskilled labor is complementary to the skilled and technical labor, while the skilled and technical labor are substitutes, with low elasticity of substitution but significantly higher than zero. This finding indicates that no consistent aggregate index of labor can be formed. These estimates are in sharp contrast to those received by Bowles (1970). Using a two-stage CES production function, this author found high elasticity of substitution among all types of labor classified by years of schooling. Elasticities with values of 6-8 were found by Bowles and Dougherty (1972) and of .61 by Fallon and Layard (1975).

These differences are partly due to differences in data and partly due to differences in specification. The two stage CES specification does not allow for complementarity, an important characteristic of our result. This complementarity relationship between human capital and raw labor has important implications for economic growth. Developing economies which have abundant unskilled labor cannot use it as a substitute for skill requirements in production. The production of human capital is a necessary condition to avoid an educational bottleneck as a barrier to economic growth.

For educational planners, the most obvious implication of the results is that both the rate of return analyses and the manpower requirements approach are based on assumptions not supported by our data. It seems that the rate of return analyses with constant relative wage rates and infinite elasticity of substitution should be more misleading than the manpower requirements approach as a tool for educational planning in Iraq.

In accounting for economic growth it is necessary to construct a labor index reflecting the growth of labor inputs over a period of time. Since the labor force is not homogenous an estimate of the elasticity of substitution will suggest a weighting scheme to create a consistent index of labor. Since our estimates are far from being infinite, the value usually assumed in the growth accounting literature (see Denison [1967]), it supports the approach taken in this paper, namely one should start from a production function in which labor of different categories appears as separate inputs.

We now proceed and analyze the capital-skill complementary hypothesis. Using the definition of capital labor substitution from Section II, X_i and K are substitutes if $\frac{\partial S_i}{\partial K} = \beta_{iK} < 0.$

$$\beta_{UK} \underset{(6.33)}{=.0328} \qquad \beta_{SK} \underset{(9.78)}{=.2105} \qquad \beta_{TK} \underset{(2.16)}{=.0071} \qquad \beta_{NK} \underset{(12.63)}{=.0956}$$

All types of labor are substitutes to capital. The strongest effect of a change in K is on the skilled labor, and the lowest is on the technical labor. Thus the most educated labor is less substitutable for capital but this relative complementarity does not hold consistently for the second ranked skill group, since the unskilled labor is less substitutable with capital than the skilled labor.

The purpose of this chapter was to study the form of technical change and its contribution to economic growth of the public industrial sector of Iraq, a country that belongs to a group of small developing countries that chose to follow a socialist path. A dual profit function has been used to model a parametric approach to the measurement of total factor productivity, biases in technical change, returns to scale and substitution elasticities.

This approach has been used as an alternative to the traditional method of estimating productivity, as a simple residual of growth in output minus growth in inputs. The empirical results indicate that productivity analyses are very sensitive to the assumptions made regarding returns to scale and the form of technical change.

We have found strong evidence for labor-saving bias in technical change in Iraq. This explains part of the reduction in the input-output values of all types of labor. The technical labor, whose input-output coefficient suffered the sharpest decline, exhibits also the stronger saving bias estimating among the labor inputs. Since human capital is still a very scarce factor in Iraq, the finding that this is the factor mostly saved by technical progress is a positive one from the point of view of economic development.

Since we found strong labor saving biases in the sub-periods 1961-63 and 1964-67, we rejected the possibility that this estimated pattern of technical change is a result of the fact that the government nationalized in 1964 the most capital intensive private firms.

The labor "saving" results gives one explanation to the conflict between output and employment observed in many LDC's. In the case of Iraq, since it does not have relatively abundant labor, it may cause less employment problems than in other LDC's.

The parametric estimation of the rate of growth of total factor productivity support our conclusions in Chapter I. The main factors explaining economic growth in Iraq are capital accumulation and labor growth. Total factor productivity, though sensitive to the assumptions made, plays a minor part in explaining output growth.

CHAPTER III

ALLOCATIVE AND TECHNICAL EFFICIENCY OF PRIVATE AND GOVERNMENT FIRMS IN IRAQ

Much attention and criticism has been given to the size and rate of growth of the public sector in the western developed countries during the post war period. On the other hand, the role of the government in developing countries in directing and implementing growth and development has been accepted in the most natural way. The assumption that in less developed countries the market mechanism is underdeveloped has been used as a justification for the role that governments have to play in the economic life of less developed countries. Many developing countries have adopted the framework of a periodical development plan as the tool to achieve development targets.

Iraq, a Middle Eastern country, is one of the developing countries which strove to become a socialist country in terms of its economic structure and the role of the government. Since the early sixties, Iraq's private industrial sector became stagnant while the size of the public sector, namely governmentally owned firms, became large enough to produce 72 percent of the total industrial production in 1975.

Despite vast expropriations of privately owned firms during the sixties, private establishments still exist in every branch of economic activity and compete with the public sector. The existence of this dual ownership in most industries raises two interesting questions: 1) the relative economic efficiency of the private versus the public sector, and 2) the issue of welfare loss occurring to the society resulting from the departure from a private competitive market system. The idea of welfare loss arises from the widespread belief that public establishments are not efficient, namely they do not produce at minimum achievable cost. A privately owned firm, it is claimed, will use economic resources more efficiently and the welfare loss will vanish.

The purpose of this study is to analyze relative economic efficiency of privately and governmentally owned firms in Iraq's manufacturing sector, while no attempt is being made here to measure the economic loss, if it does exist. The concept of economic efficiency is broken into three parts: 1) technical efficiency, 2) price efficiency, and 3) policy efficiency. These three concepts are discussed in the following section and are incorporated into a model of firm behavior developed below. This model will be used to study relative economic efficiency. The main features of the model are that firms do not have the same production function, and profit maximization is not a maintained hypothesis. In building the model, we make use of the stochastic production function concept introduced by Zellner et al. (1966) and also incorporate the concept of restricted profit function that has been used by Lau and Yotopoulos (1971) and (1973) to study economic efficiency of Indian agriculture. The neoclassical assumption that firms maximize return has been challenged, specifically in the context of less developed countries, which have a different social and institutional setting than the advanced countries for which the concept of maximizing profit has been developed. This hypothesis, sometimes named as the rationality hypothesis, has been tested mainly in the agriculture sector of less developed countries and yielded mixed results. Wise and Yotopoulos (1969) and Lau and Yotopoulos (1973), failed to reject the hypothesis while earlier studies by Hopper (1966), Welch (1965) and Sahota (1968) rejected it.[1] We extend the hypothesis of allocative efficiency to conclude also technical

---

[1]Wise and Yotopoulos (1969) give a detailed analysis of the maximization of return hypothesis and summarize past tests.

efficiency and test it for firms in the industrial sector of a developing country.

The analytical framework developed in the next section is used to study relative economic efficiency of private and government firms in the food, mineral and chemical industries of Iraq. Our results reveal that output of private firms could be increased if all firms achieved those levels of technical efficiency that were in fact achieved by firms who belong to the government sector. An additional gain in output can be obtained if the large allocation inefficiencies found in government firms will be eliminated.

Theoretical Framework

Technical Efficiency

The theoretical definition of a production function as expressing the maximum amount of output obtainable from given bundles of variable and fixed inputs has been made econometrically operational by two widely used assumptions: (1) all firms within an industry share the same technology (have the same production function); (2) firms have a deterministic and known production function. The first assumption, implying that all firms are equally technically efficient, led to the practice of using cross section data on the level of output and inputs for firms within an industry and of estimating an average production function for the industry.

The observation that firms within an industry are not equally technically efficient (that is, produce different levels of output with the same set of inputs) revealed that more information can be obtained from production data by estimating so called frontier production functions or best practice functions. The work of Farrell (1957) was a first attempt to measure technical efficiency, using the frontier notion, and it was followed by the work of Aigner and Chu

(1968), Afriat (1972) and Richmond (1974). These studies used mathematical linear programming methods to estimate the technical relationship, minimizing the difference between actual output and its estimated value subject to the constraint that the estimated values always exceed or are equal to the actual ones. The estimated technology represents the frontier which is always greater than or equal to any of the actually observed values of output. Since this approach is extremely sensitive to outliers, it has led to the development of the so called probabilistic frontier. Timmer (1971) used mathematical programming techniques except that he allowed some specified proportion of the observations to lie above the frontier. This proportion is chosen arbitrarily without much, if any, support from economic theory. Furthermore, this approach does not provide statistical properties of parameter estimates such as their standard errors and distributions.

In recent studies a truncated random error term has been introduced into the production function. Schmidt (1976) used a one-sided error term (truncated at zero and allowed to take on only non-positive values), while Aigner, Lovell and Schmidt (1977) used a two component error term to allow downward deviations from the frontier and to make the frontier stochastic.

The approach taken in this paper to study technical efficiency in a frontier framework is much simplier and more intuitively appealing than the approaches discussed above. It has its roots in the stochastic production function by Zellner et al. (1966). A deterministic version of the approach has been used implicitly by Lau and Yotopoulos (1971) and (1973) although they did not introduce the frontier concept explicitly.

It is assumed that all firms within an industry have identical stochastic production functions up to a neutral disembodied technical efficiency parameter. The production function can be written as:

$$V_i = A_i(t)\ g(x,\ z,\ u_i) \qquad i = 1,\ldots,n \tag{3.1}$$

where V_i is output of the ith firm, A_i the technical efficiency parameter is a function of time, and g the input function which is common to all firms, has as arguments a vector of variable inputs x, a vector of fixed inputs z, and a random term, u_i. A distinction should be made between the theoretical concept of technical efficiency and its implementation counterpart. A few reasons why firms vary in their ability to utilize the best practice technology at time t_0 (that is, why $A_i(t_0)$ varies over firms) are: pure technical-engineering advantage on the side of some firms, the speed of implementing new knowledge of best practice technology, namely technological change over time, systematic human errors that differ over firms according to the quality and motivation of management, the composition of capital equipment when new vintages of capital may be more technically efficient.

Only the first two reasons are included in the theoretical concept of technical efficiency. The remaining reasons are a result of our inability to specify management, quality of management, and different vintages of capital as distinct inputs (mainly because of lack of data). However, if we were able to introduce the above factors in the g function, part of the difference among firms in $A_i(t)$ will probably vanish. In this study the implementation concept of technical efficiency is being used.

The input function g is stochastic, since it includes a random element u_i which is introduced to allow for random factors that affect output such as weather, luck, machine performance, non-systematic human error, etc. The frontier production function consists of the common input function g, multiplied by the A_i with the highest value. It will be a stochastic frontier since g is stochastic. Firms whose A_i's are scattered near the frontier may land above it or below it since the disturbance term u_i can take either positive or negative values. Firms can be scaled in terms of technical efficiency using an index such as $\frac{A_i}{A^h}$ where A^h stands for the frontier value. To be able to discriminate among firms and identify a specific firm's technical parameter, we need more than a single cross section of data.

The Objective Function and Allocative Efficiency

Neoclassical theory of production postulates that firms in a competitive market will derive their optimal amount of inputs from the objective of maximizing profits. Therefore a firm is allocative efficient if it equates the value of the marginal product of each variable input to its opportunity cost. It has been acknowledged in the literture that this optimality condition may not hold strictly and more than random deviation from optimality should be allowed in empirical implementation of the theory (Hoch [1958], Mundlak [1963]). This issue gains more importance when speaking of developing economies, especially the so called socialist developing countries where much of the production sector is state owned and managed by government officials.

Marginal productivity of factors may deviate from their cost because of consistent mistakes regarding prices of factors and outputs. Marginal productivity may include a return to the firm as a compensation for on-the-job training provided to its employees. Further, the objective of a governmentally owned and operated firm may not be maximization of profits. A government concerned with industrialization may give its firms targets such as output quotas, growth of capital invested in the firm, employment targets and so on. This will result in what we call policy inefficiency. From the point of view of competitive market theory, there is a misallocation of economic resources but it may be justified in terms of the government's objective function. Although policy inefficiency is conceptually different from allocative inefficiency, they cannot be separated analytically since both result in marginal productivities of factors being different from their respective opportunity costs.

To introduce allocative and policy inefficiency into firms' behavior without specifying explicitly an objective function different from profit maximization, we allow firms to be unsuccessful in their attempts to equate values of marginal products of inputs to their respective prices by introducing the following general systematic rule of behavior: firms equate the value of the marginal product of factors to a constant proportion of the firms factors prices.[1] For a typical firm:

$$P \frac{\partial V_i}{\partial x_i} = k_i w_i \qquad i = 1,\ldots,n$$

(here the ith subscript stands for the ith variable input). A perfect profit maximization is a special case when $k_i = 1$. This kind of behavior can be rationalized as follows: consistent under or over valuation of costs of factor of production to the firm, non-profit maximizing behavior, mistakes in predicting the output price. An alternative way to look at the problem is to treat $k_i w_i$ as the effective prices facing the firm, the prices that the firm uses in its profit maximization considerations.

A Simple Model of the Firm

A typical firm is assumed to have a Cobb-Douglas[2] production function with decreasing return to scale, given in (3.2):

$$\text{(3.2)} \qquad V_i = A_i(t) x^{\alpha} z^{\beta} e^{u_i} \qquad i = 1,\ldots,n$$

---

[1] This approach has been introduced in the literature first by Hoch (1955) and used also by Bruno (1968), Lau and Yotopoulos (1971) and Lau and Yotopoulos (1973).

[2] The Cobb-Douglas form is used here since it fits well the data and it also allows us to derive its exact dual profit function. It is possible to derive the same model using a generalized production function to allow return to scale not to be constant.

For simplicity of notation the function is specified with one variable input x and one fixed input z. The generalization of the analyses to many inputs is straightforward. n is the number of firms in the industry.

The entrepreneur is aware of the stochastic behavior of V_i which results in uncertain profits. Variable profits given in (3.3) are defined as value of output less total variable cost:

$$\Pi_i = V_i P - kwx \,. \tag{3.3}$$

Assuming that the firm determines the value of x and that w is given to the firm and is non-stochastic, equation (3.3) has two stochastic elements, V_i and P, where P is a random variable correlated with V_i, since it is a function of aggregate output $V_a = \sum_i^n V_i$ that depends on u_i.

Following Zellner et al. (1966) it is assumed that the entrepreneur maximizes the mathematical expectation of profit given in (3.4):

$$E(\Pi_i) = E\left[V_i(A_i, x, z, u_i)P(V_a, u_i)\right] - k_i w_i x \tag{3.4}$$

where E denotes mathematical expectation. Iraq is a socialist country and the government effectively controls the price system. In other words, the government determines the prices of products. Furthermore, for the period 1961-1968, with which the empirical work to be reported below is concerned, the nominal prices of all products included in the study were constant. Data on monthly wholesale prices for these years shows no variation at all. Under this price control system, it is reasonable to assume that producers know in advance the prices of their product. P becomes non-stochastic and each firm faces an infinitely elastic demand for its output.[1] The market will be in equilibrium,

[1] Grossman (1975) developed a complete model, where V and P are stochastic. In his model, expectations are formed rationally and a Bayesian procedure was used to develop an econometric model.

given that the government sets prices at their market clearing value.

Some complications arise if P_g, the government fixed price, is different from the free market equilibrium price, P^e. In Figure 1, S^p, S^g, and S^{p+g} are the private, government and total supply curves respectively, and D is the demand curve facing the industry.

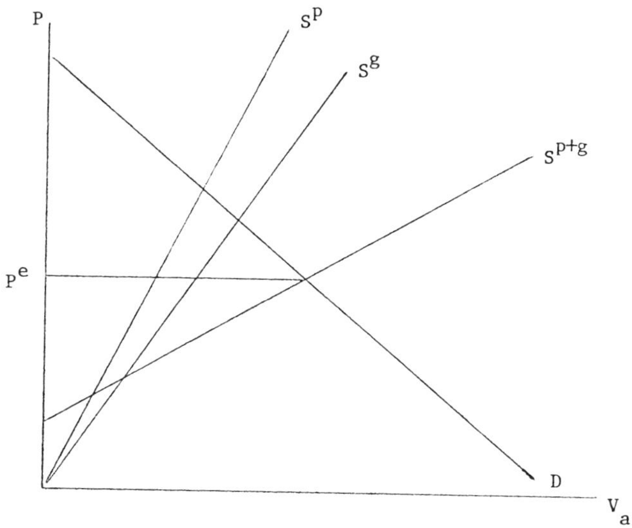

Fig. 1--Domestic demand and supply curves.

If $P^g < P^e$, then an unsatisfied excess demand will have to be cleared by some rationing system. The case when $P^g > P^e$ is less realistic since most manufacturing products are also imported by Iraq at a world price P^w, generally higher than the domestic price P^g (part of the difference $P^w - P^g$, reflects quality differences between domestic and imported goods). In this case the supply curve facing domestic consumers will be discontinuous as shown by the curve S in Figure 2.

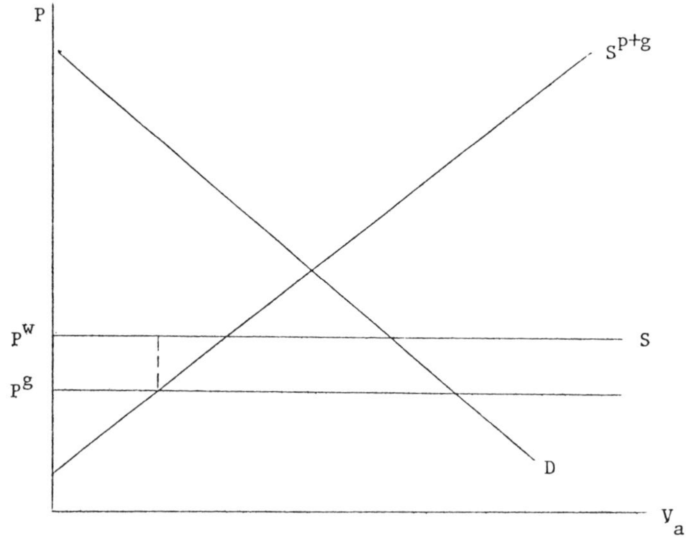

Fig. 2--Free trade equilibrium.

The market is cleared by two different prices requiring a rationing system to determine who is allowed to buy the domestic product at the lower price P^g, and who buys the imported product at the higher world price P^w. Thus, as firms take P as given, (3.4) is simplified to:

$$(3.5) \qquad E(\Pi_i) = PE(V_i) - k_i w_i x \qquad i = 1,\ldots,n$$

Assuming that the disturbance in the production function is normally distributed, deflating (3.5) by P and substituting for $E(V_i)$ in (3.5), we get the following expected unit profit identity:

$$(3.6) \qquad E(\Pi_i) = A_i x^\alpha z^\beta e^{\sigma_u^2/2} - k_i w_i x$$

where σ_u^2 is the variance of the production function disturbance. Maximizing expected profit yields the following first order condition:

$$\frac{\partial E(\Pi_i)}{\partial x} = A_i x^{\alpha-2} z^{\beta} e^{\sigma_u^2/2} - k_i w_i = 0 \qquad i = 1,\ldots,n$$

or

$$(3.7) \qquad x = \frac{\alpha E(V_i)}{k_i w_i} .$$

Equation (3.7) determines the optional quantity of the variable input to be used in production. Since firms may not be completely successful in their cost minimization efforts, an error term ε_i is incorporated exponentially in equation (3.7) to allow x^d to deviate randomly from its optimal value. By further substituting $V_i e^{\sigma_u^2/2} e^{-u_i}$ for $E(V_i)$, equation (3.7) becomes:

$$(3.7') \qquad x^d = \frac{\alpha V}{kw} e^{\sigma_0 + \varepsilon - u}$$

where $\sigma_0 = \sigma_u^2/2$. We should note that x^d in equation (3.7) is deterministic while x^d in (3.7') is stochastic. Equation (3.7') implies that the deviation of marginal productivity of variable inputs from their opportunity cost results from systematic mistakes (k) and random mistakes (ε) made in the optimal allocation of inputs.

Using the stochastic production function (3.2) the stochastic first order condition (3.7') and the actual unit profit identity $\Pi_i = V_i - wx$, we derive the stochastic profit function (3.8), variable input demand function (3.9), and the output supply function (3.10).[1]

$$(3.8) \qquad \Pi = A_i^{\frac{1}{1-\alpha}} k_i^{-\frac{\alpha}{1-\alpha}} \alpha^{\frac{\alpha}{1-\alpha}} e^{\frac{\alpha}{1-\alpha}\sigma_0} w^{-\frac{\alpha}{1-\alpha}} z^{\frac{\beta}{1-\alpha}} (1 - \frac{\alpha}{k} e^{\sigma_0+\varepsilon_i-u_i}) e^{(\frac{\alpha}{1-\alpha})\varepsilon_i + u_i}$$

---

[1]The stochastic production function (3.2) and the stochastic first order condition (3.7') are structural equations which together with actual unit profit identity form a simultaneous equation system. The profit, output supply and input demand functions given by (3.8), (3.7) and (3.10) respectively are the reduced form system of the model (the algebraic solution for the endogenous variables).

$$(3.9) \qquad x^d = A_i^{\frac{1}{1-\alpha}} k_i^{-\frac{1}{1-\alpha}} \alpha^{\frac{1}{1-\alpha}} e^{\frac{\alpha}{1-\alpha}\sigma_0} w^{-\frac{1}{1-\alpha}} z^{\frac{\beta}{1-\alpha}} e^{(\frac{1}{1-\alpha})\varepsilon_i}$$

$$(3.10) \qquad V^s = A_i^{\frac{1}{1-\alpha}} k_i^{-\frac{\alpha}{1-\alpha}} \alpha^{\frac{\alpha}{1-\alpha}} e^{\frac{\alpha}{1-\alpha}\sigma_0} w^{-\frac{\alpha}{1-\alpha}} z^{\frac{\beta}{1-\alpha}} e^{(\frac{\alpha}{1-\alpha})\varepsilon_i + u_i}$$

The profit and supply functions involve two random terms: u_i--the output disturbance and ε_i--the variable input demand disturbance. On the other hand, the input demand function given in (3.9), includes only the ε_i term since x^d is distributed independently of the disturbance term u_i of the production function. This is the result of making x^d a control variable to the firm which maximizes the mathematical expectations of profits.

Assuming that technical progress is Hicks-neutral, we specify $A_{it} = A_{i0}e^{\lambda_{it}}$ where t is time and λ_i is the exogenous measure of technical change.

We rewrite equations (3.8) - (3.10) as:

$$(3.8') \qquad \Pi = B_i^{\pi} e^{(\frac{\lambda_i}{1-\alpha})t} w^{-\frac{\alpha}{1-\alpha}} z^{\frac{\beta}{1-\alpha}} G_i e^{(\frac{\alpha}{1-\alpha})\varepsilon_i + u_i}$$

$$(3.9') \qquad x^d = B_i^{x} e^{(\frac{\lambda_i}{1-\alpha})t} w^{-\frac{1}{1-\alpha}} z^{\frac{\beta}{1-\alpha}} e^{(\frac{1}{1-\alpha})\varepsilon_i}$$

$$(3.10') \qquad V^s = B_i^{v} e^{(\frac{\lambda_i}{1-\alpha})t} w^{-\frac{\alpha}{1-\alpha}} z^{\frac{\beta}{1-\alpha}} e^{(\frac{\alpha}{1-\alpha})\varepsilon_i + u_i}$$

where:

$$B_i^{\pi} = A_{0i}^{\frac{1}{1-\alpha}} k_i^{\frac{\alpha}{1-\alpha}} \alpha^{\frac{\alpha}{1-\alpha}} e^{\frac{\alpha}{1-\alpha}\sigma_0}$$

$$(3.11) \qquad B_i^{x} = A_{0i}^{\frac{1}{1-\alpha}} k_i^{-\frac{1}{1-\alpha}} \alpha^{\frac{1}{1-\alpha}} e^{\frac{1}{1-\alpha}\sigma_0}$$

$$B_i^{v} = A_{0i}^{\frac{1}{1-\alpha}} k_i^{-\frac{\alpha}{1-\alpha}} \alpha^{\frac{\alpha}{1-\alpha}} e^{\frac{\alpha}{1-\alpha}\sigma_0}$$

$$G_i = 1 - \frac{\alpha}{k_i} e^{\sigma_0 + \varepsilon - u}$$

Each equation in the system (3.8') - (3.10') has a part common to all firms and two components that vary over firms. The parameters α and β, the coefficients of the wages of variable inputs, and the level of fixed inputs (which vary across firms) are common to all firms. The parameters that vary across firms are the rate of technological change λ_i and the constant terms in each equation defined in (3.11). Each constant is a function of the technical efficiency parameter, A_i, the allocative efficiency parameter, k_i, and σ_u^2, the variance of the production function random term. If firms have different A_0's, λ's or k's, this will be reflected in variation across firms in the value of B^π, B^x and B^v. In the next section we make use of these constant terms to formulate the economic efficiency hypotheses that we are interested in to test.

Formulation of Hypotheses to be Tested

The system (3.8') - (3.10') is used as the basis for the empirical work in this study. Estimation can be carried out using only two of the three equations since the profit identity makes one equation redundant. To derive the various hypotheses of relative economic efficiency, it is useful to use the input demand function and output supply function and to drop the profit function since it has a complicated non-linear error term structure. Thus, the following formulation of the hypotheses are unique to the pair of equations used.

The first hypothesis that we are interested in testing is that of equal relative economic efficiency of governmentally and privately owned firms within the same industry. This will hold if the two firms have an identical supply function, which is satisfied if:

$$(3.12) \qquad B_g^v = B_p^v$$

where g and p stand for government and private firm, respectively. No constraint is imposed on λ_g, λ_p, A_{0g}, A_{0p}, k_g and k_p since the condition expressed by (3.12) can be satisfied without the firms being equally technically or price efficient.

Two firms are equally technically and price efficient if $A_{0g} = A_{0p}$, $\lambda_g = \lambda_p$, $k_g = k_p$. A sufficient condition in order for this to be satisfied is

$$(3.13) \qquad B_g^x = B_p^x \qquad B_g^v = B_p^v \qquad \text{and} \qquad \lambda_p = \lambda_g \ .$$

The restrictions expressed in (3.13) can be tested as a joint hypothesis.

An important question is which firm is doing better in terms of equalizing the value of marginal product to the price of factors? If the two firms are equally allocatively efficient, namely $k_p = k_g$, it implies that

$$(3.14) \qquad \frac{B_g^v}{B_p^v} = \left(\frac{A_{0g}}{A_{op}}\right)^{\frac{1}{1-\alpha}} \qquad \frac{B_g^x}{B_p^x} = \left(\frac{A_{0g}}{A_{0p}}\right)^{\frac{1}{1-\alpha}}$$

The equality of the right hand terms of the expressions in (3.14) implies

$$(3.15) \qquad \frac{B_g^v}{B_p^v} = \frac{A_g^x}{A_p^x}$$

which is a sufficient test for the hypothesis $k_p = k_g$.

A sufficient and necessary condition for each firm to be a perfect profit maximizer is that k = 1. For a government firm this condition will also imply that there isn't any evidence for policy inefficiency regarding the variable input. If k = 1, then the ratio of the output supply and labor demands constant terms can be written as

$$(3.16) \qquad \frac{B_g^x}{A_g^v} = \alpha e^{\sigma_0} \qquad \frac{B_p^x}{B_p^v} = \alpha e^{\sigma_0}$$

which can be used as a necessary and sufficient statistical test of the hypothesis of profit maximization. It can be applied to each firm separately ($k_g = 1$ or $k_p = 1$) or to both firms jointly ($k_g = k_p = 1$).

A set of duality theorems proven in McFadden (1965) and Lau (1968) established relations between the production function and the profit function. All the production functions parameters can be estimated indirectly by estimating directly the profit function (or its counterpart, the supply and factor demand functions). The duality relations were established for a deterministic model. In the stochastic framework developed above, an additional parameter σ_u with an unknown value is introduced. An estimate for σ_u^2 can be obtained from the residuals of the output supply and input demand functions and used in testing the profit maximization hypothesis (k = 1) given in equation (3.16). Furthermore, $\hat{\sigma}_u$ can be used to derive estimates for A_{0i} from the constants B_i^x and B_i^v.

To carry out these tests we chose x^d (3.9') and V^s (3.10') as the equations to be estimated. After taking natural logarithms of equations (3.9') and (3.10'), we get:

$$(3.17) \qquad \ell n\ x^d = \ell n\ B_i^x + \frac{\lambda_i}{1-\alpha}t - \frac{1}{1-\alpha}\ \ell n\ w + \frac{p}{1-\alpha}\ \ell n\ z + \frac{1}{1-\alpha}\ \varepsilon$$

$$(3.18) \qquad \ell n\ V^s = \ell n\ B_i^v + \frac{\lambda_i}{1-\alpha}t - \frac{\alpha}{1-\alpha}\ \ell n\ w + \frac{\beta}{1-\alpha}\ \ell n\ z + \frac{\alpha}{1-\alpha}\ \varepsilon + u$$

These two equations have non-stochastic variables on the right hand side (w and z) but they share common parameters α, β and λ, resulting in the familiar equality restrictions that should be imposed on the system. Furthermore, the hypotheses derived above involve cross equation restrictions. We thus have to use a multivariate regression method to estimate the system. Since ε_i appears in the error term of each equation, we can expect a gain in estimation efficiency by estimating the two equations simultaneously.

Application to Iraq

This section will report the results of studying relative economic efficiency of governmental versus private owned firms for three industries: food, chemical and mineral product industry. Because of the small size of the samples available, we assume that within an industry, government firms are identical to each other in terms of the A_0, λ and k. The same assumption is made regarding the private firms. Thus, we actually compare a typical government firm to a typical private firm when both produce a roughly homogeneous product.

The data used in this study is obtained by pooling time series (1961-1968) and cross section observations of firms within each industry. A brief description of the variables and the notation used is as follows:[1]

V = a value added measure of physical output per firm (value added deflated by the price of output).

x = the labor input per firm measured in hours of work. It includes non-paid workers.

z = a measure of flow of capital services per firm, assumed to be the fixed factor in production.

w = the hourly wage of labor in Iraqi Dinnars deflated by output price. It includes imputed wages to non-paid workers and employees benefits not included in the wage bill.

Π = the unit output profit of the firm: total revenue less total variable labor costs, deflated by output price.[2]

---

[1] A more detailed description of the data is given in the Appendix.

[2] I used the price of output reported in the annual abstract of statistics.

We rewrite the labor demand equation (3.17) and the output supply equation (3.18), specifying specific constants and time variables to each type of firm. Hence, our final estimating equations consist of:

$$(3.19) \qquad \ell n\, x^d = \theta_p D_p + \theta_g D_g + \lambda_p^* t_p + \lambda_g^* t_g - \bar{\alpha}\, \ell n\, w + \beta^* \, \ell n\, z + e_1$$

$$(3.20) \qquad \ell n\, V^s = \delta_p D_p + \delta_g D_g + \lambda_p^* t_p + \lambda_g^* t_g - \alpha^* \, \ell n\, w + \beta^* \, \ell n\, z + e_2$$

where

$$\lambda^* = \frac{\lambda}{1-\alpha} \qquad \bar{\alpha} = \frac{1}{1-\alpha} \qquad \alpha^* = \frac{\alpha}{1-\alpha} \qquad \beta^* = \frac{\beta}{1-\alpha}$$

$$e_1 = \left(\frac{1}{1-\alpha}\right) \qquad e_2 = \left(\frac{\alpha}{1-\alpha}\right)\varepsilon + u$$

and D_p and D_g are dummy variables taking the value of one for government and private firms, respectively, and zero otherwise. θ_p and θ_g, δ_p and δ_g are the private and the government intercept coefficients of the labor demand and output supply functions, respectively.

We assume that $e = (e_1, e_2)$ has a bivariate normal distribution and allow the covariance of the errors of the two equations to be non-zero for a given firm. However, the covariances of the errors of either equation corresponding to different firms are assumed to be zero. Furthermore, it is assumed that the disturbances in each equation are not correlated over time.

The estimation of (3.19) and (3.20) involve cross equations non-linear equality restrictions. Furthermore, some of the hypotheses to be tested also involve non-linear restrictions. We used a full information maximum likelihood estimation computer program[1] that allows for non-linear restrictions. Since we

---

As indicated in the previous section the monthly and annual prices were very stable probably as a result of government regulation. If private firms manage to obtain higher prices for their product, by using lower price index, we over-estimate the output of private firms.

[1] I have used the Resimul program developed by C. Wymer which is designed

obtain maximum likelihood estimates, we may test whether or not the loss of fit from imposing restrictions is significant by using the likelihood ratio test. Denoting the determinants of the unrestricted and restricted estimates of the disturbance covariance matrix by $|\hat{\Omega}_r|$ and $|\hat{\Omega}_u|$ respectively, we can write the likelihood ratio as $\lambda = [(|\hat{\Omega}_r|)/(|\hat{\Omega}_u|)]^{n/2}$ where n is the number of observations. The statistic (-2) $\ell n\ \lambda$, computed to test all restrictions, is distributed asymptotically as chi-squared with degrees of freedom equal to the number of independent restrictions being imposed.

The set of hypotheses to be tested for each industry are:

(1) The hypothesis of equal relative economic efficiency of government and private firms is expressed by the condition given in (3.12):

$$H_0: \delta_p = \delta_g$$

(2) The joint hypothesis of equal technical and allocative efficiency is expressed by condition (3.13):

$$H_0: \theta_p = \theta_g \qquad \delta_p = \delta_g \qquad \lambda_p^* = \lambda_g^*$$

(3) The hypothesis of equal allocative efficiency with respect to labor demand is expressed by condition (3.15):

$$H_0: \delta_g - \theta_g = \delta_p - \theta_p$$

(4) The hypothesis of absolute allocative efficiency of private firms ($k_p = 1$) given by equation (3.17):

$$H_0: \theta_p - \delta_p = \ell n\ \alpha + \hat{\sigma}_0$$

---

to obtain full information maximum likelihood estimates of a system that contains non-linear restrictions within and across equations. The program follows a Newton-Raphson iterative procedure, beginning with arbitrarily given initial values of the parameters.

(5) The hypothesis of absolute allocative efficiency of government firms ($k_g = 1$):

$$H_0: \theta_g - \delta_g = \ell n \alpha + \hat{\sigma}_0$$

Tables 5, 6 and 7 present parameter estimates of equations (3.19) and (3.20) for the three industries, under different maintained hypotheses. The equality restrictions are imposed and used as part of the basic model. To make sure that the maximum of likelihood function obtained is indeed a global maximum, we started with different initial values for the parameters. The convergence of the system to the same parameter values for all the sets of equations estimated guarantees that the likelihood value obtained is the global maximum.

A well behaved restricted profit function has to be decreasing and convex in the wage rate and increasing in the value of fixed input, capital. From the equality of parameters implied by the system (3.8') - (3.10'), the input demand and output supply functions should also be decreasing and convex in the wage rate and increasing in the capital value. The coefficient of the wage rate is negative while the coefficient of capital is positive in all equations, in accord with a priori economic theory.

The precision of the point estimates in Tables 5, 6 and 7 is satisfactory except for the constants θ and δ in the chemical industry, which have large standard errors. Therefore, we should be cautious when we interpret the results of the chemical industry.

Table 6 summarizes the results of testing five hypotheses for each industry. The first hypothesis of equal relative economic efficiency is rejected for the food and mineral industries and it is accepted for the chemical industry.[1]

---

[1]We should be cautious in interpreting the likelihood ratio test results as definitive: different asymptotically equivalent testing procedures may, in finite samples, yield conflicting decisions regarding the acceptance or rejection of the null hypothesis. See for example Berndt and Savin (1977).

TABLE 6

FOOD INDUSTRY: RESULTS OF JOINT ESTIMATION OF DEMAND FOR LABOR AND OUTPUT SUPPLY UNDER VARIOUS HYPOTHESES
(asymptotic t values in parentheses)

Parameter	Basic Model	Maintained Hypothesis				
		EREE	EAE and ETE	EAE	$k_g = 1$	$k_p = 1$
θ_g	5.89 (4.95)	4.47 (3.83)	1.90 (1.32)	5.89 (5.18)	6.81 (9.66)	5.17 (6.31)
θ_p	5.06 (4.75)	4.73 (4.07)	. . .	5.07 (4.75)	5.92 (9.36)	4.37 (5.82)
λ_g^*	.06 (1.20)	.16 (3.71)	-.00 (.01)	.06 (1.20)	.05 (1.05)	.06 (1.31)
λ_p^*	-.06 (1.33)	-.16 (3.70)	. . .	-.06 (1.33)	-.07 (1.42)	-.06 (1.26)
$\bar{\alpha}$	1.72 (8.88)	1.81 (8.64)	1.99 (7.03)	1.72 (8.88)	1.54 (23.9)	1.86 (17.4)
β^*	.20 (3.23)	.26 (3.91)	.46 (5.99)	.20 (3.23)	.16 (3.23)	.23 (4.35)
δ_g	7.00 (6.25)	5.50 (4.72)	2.79 (1.94)	6.79 (5.96)	7.87 (10.6)	6.24 (7.58)
δ_p	5.79 (5.43)	. . .	. . .	5.97 (5.58)	6.66 (10.42)	5.14 (6.45)
α^*	.72 (3.71)	.81 (3.88)	.99 (3.51)	.72 (3.71)	.54 (8.33)	.86 (8.06)
Var. (e_1)	.22	.26	.53	.22	.23	.22
Var. (e_2)	.40	.41	.89	.44	.42	.40
Cov. $(e_1 e_2)$	.23	.25	.61	.23	.24	.22

Notes: EREE = Equal Relative Economic Efficiency.
EAE = Equal Relative Allocative Efficiency.
ETE = Equal Relative Technical Efficiency.
The number of observations equals 52.

TABLE 7

MINERAL INDUSTRY: RESULTS OF JOINT ESTIMATION OF DEMAND FOR LABOR AND OUTPUT SUPPLY UNDER VARIOUS HYPOTHESES
(asymptotic t values in parentheses)

Parameter	Basic Model	Maintained Hypothesis: EREE	EAE and ETE	EAE	$k_g = 1$	$k_p = 1$
θ_g	5.94 (5.00)	5.26 (4.30)	3.43 (2.43)	5.85 (4.88)	5.11 (3.20)	5.82 (7.71)
θ_p	5.49 (4.75)	5.38 (4.46)	. . .	5.58 (4.82)	4.35 (3.12)	5.37 (7.18)
λ^*_g	.06 (1.39)	.11 (2.84)	.05 (1.43)	.06 (1.39)	.06 (1.39)	.06 (1.50)
λ^*_p	-.07 (1.49)	-.09 (2.01)	. . .	-.07 (1.49)	-.06 (1.42)	-.06 (1.51)
$\bar{\alpha}$	1.76 (5.74)	1.79 (5.61)	1.70 (4.36)	1.76 (5.74)	1.73 (4.90)	1.80 (11.3)
β^*	.23 (6.15)	.25 (6.43)	.41 (10.4)	.23 (6.15)	.23 (5.25)	.24 (7.35)
δ_g	7.17 (5.82)	.634 (5.20)	4.45 (3.14)	6.86 (5.69)	6.35 (5.56)	7.05 (9.08)
δ_p	6.29 (5.41)	. . .	. . .	6.60 (5.66)	6.05 (5.20)	6.18 (7.35)
α^*	.76 (2.48)	.79 (2.47)	.70 (1.79)	.76 (2.48)	.76 (2.35)	.80 (4.99)
Var. (e_1)	.15	.15	.16	.16	.16	.15
Var. (e_2)	.67	.70	.51	.76	.77	.67
Cov. (e_1e_2)	.27	.27	.17	.30	.26	2.7

Notes: See Table 6.
The number of observations equals 32.

TABLE 8

CHEMICAL INDUSTRY: RESULTS OF JOINT ESTIMATION OF DEMAND FOR LABOR AND OUTPUT SUPPLY UNDER VARIOUS HYPOTHESES
(asymptotic t values in parentheses)

Parameter	Basic Model	Maintained Hypothesis				
		EREE	EAE and ETE	EAE	$k_g = 1$	$k_p = 1$
θ_g	.70 (.55)	.47 (.40)	.36 (.21)	.80 (.54)	.60 (.54)	.58 (.49)
θ_p	.64 (.53)	.69 (.58)	. . .	.59 (.50)	.54 (.44)	.51 (.46)
λ_g^*	.12 (.74)	.153 (.60)	.07 (1.23)	.12 (.74)	.13 (1.02)	.11 (1.02)
λ_p^*	-.02 (.54)	-.02 (.60)	. . .	-.02 (.54)	-.02 (.51)	-.03 (.53)
$\bar{\alpha}$	2.28 (5.70)	2.26 (5.75)	1.75 (3.28)	2.28 (5.70)	1.85 (4.50)	1.91 (4.70)
β^*	.62 (13.7)	.62 (13.7)	.71 (11.7)	.62 (13.7)	.68 (12.5)	.66 (11.9)
δ_g	1.65 (1.80)	1.64 (1.82)	1.24 (1.12)	1.70 (1.56)	1.35 (1.54)	1.45 (1.64)
δ_p	1.42 (1.76)	. . .	. . .	1.50 (1.77)	1.12 (1.65)	1.22 (1.75)
α^*	1.28 (3.20)	1.26 (3.21)	.75 (1.41)	1.28 (3.20)	.85 (3.30)	.91 (4.2)
Var. (e_1)	.20	.20	.30	.20	.25	.21
Var. (e_2)	.14	.14	.27	.14	.22	.19
Cov. (e_1e_2)	.08	.08	.20	.08	.15	.16

Notes: See Table 6.
The number of observations equals 28.

The likelihood ratio test statistics are 9.69 and 5.32 for the food and mineral industries respectively, above 3.84 and 5.02, the critical values at the .05 and .025 significance level. The point estimate for δ_g, which is significantly higher than δ_p, reveal the interesting result that on the whole, government firms are more economically efficient than private firms in the food and mineral industries. In other words, for the given wages paid and capital services used by the firms in the sample, the supply curve of an average government firm lies above the private average curve. Furthermore, the two kinds of firms differ significantly in the components of economic efficiency. The joint hypothesis of equal allocative and technical efficiency is rejected for the three industries while the hypothesis of equal allocative efficiency is rejected for food and mineral industries.

We proceed to test the hypothesis of perfect profit maximization in both sectors for each industry. The allocative efficiency hypothesis has been examined in few studies of the traditional agriculture sector of developing economies. It has been first formulated by T. W. Schultz (1964), p. 37):

> There are comparatively few significant inefficiencies in the allocation of the factors of production in traditional agriculture.

Earlier studies do not support the hypothesis that peasant agriculture is highly allocatively efficient (see Hopper, 1966; Chennareddy, 1967, Welsch, 1965 and Sahota, 1968). On the contrary, all these studies found significant deviations from optimal resource allocation. Recent studies by Lau and Yotopoulos (1973) and Sidhu (1974) support the hypothesis: they have found that both large and small forms in Indian agriculture are allocatively efficient.

No empirical evidence is available regarding technical and allocative efficiency in the industrial sector of developing economies despite the important role that industrial growth has in development plans in many of these countries. From the result presented in Tables 8 and 9, there seems to be significant possibilities for growth in Iraq by improving allocative efficiency in government firms and improving technical efficiency in private firms by moving toward production frontiers.

TABLE 9

TESTING OF STATISTICAL HYPOTHESES

	Degrees of Freedom	Critical χ^2 .05	Critical χ^2 .025	Likelihood Ratio Food	Likelihood Ratio Mineral	Likelihood Ratio Chemical
$\delta_p = \delta_g$	1	3.84	5.02	9.69	5.32	.06
$\delta_p = \delta_g$, $\theta_p = \theta_g$, $\lambda^*_p = \lambda^*_g$	3	7.81	9.35	51.24	20.40	21.35
$\delta_g - \theta_g = \delta_p - \theta_p$	1	3.84	5.02	8.47	4.90	1.6
$\theta_p - \delta_p = \ell n\ \alpha + \hat{\sigma}_0$	1	3.84	5.02	.78	3.51	7.12
$\theta_g - \delta_g = \ell n\ \alpha + \hat{\sigma}_0$	1	3.84	5.02	5.73	9.74	10.21

TABLE 10

EFFICIENCY PARAMETER ESTIMATES

	Food	Mineral	Chemical
k_p	1.0	1.21	2.01
k_g	1.42	1.95	2.51
$\frac{A_{0g}}{A_{0p}}$	1.42	1.15	1.0

Notes: k is computed using the following formula:

$$k = \frac{B^v}{B^x} \alpha e^{\sigma_0}$$

σ_0 is computed using the following formula:

$$\sigma_0 = \left[\text{Var } e_2 - \alpha^2 \text{ Var } e_1\right]/2$$

The hypothesis of perfect profit maximization cannot be rejected for the private food and mineral industries. k_p is equal to one in the food industry and equal to 1.21, but not significantly different from one in the mineral industry. On the other hand, we observe clear evidence of deviation from perfect profit maximization in the behavior of government firms.

It reveals sizable allocation inefficiencies since the ratio of value of marginal product to wages paid to labor ranges from 1.42 in the food industry to 2.51 in the chemical industry. Allocative inefficiency exists also in the private chemical industry. Thus, government firms in all three industries are not using labor at its optimum value: the value of marginal product of labor is above the wage rate. Using less labor than is optimal, implies that firms use too much of other factors of production, mainly capital. This indicates very considerable systematic overcapitalization in government firms. It is very probable that the cost of capital to a government firm is lower than its social opportunity cost because of cheap loans or lower energy prices. The distorted factor price ratio causes the capital labor ratio to be higher than its optimal value. The overcapitalization in the government sector is consistent with the observation that capital labor ratios are higher at these government firms compared to the private ones. More on-the-job training provided by government firms in an attempt to upgrade the productivity of the labor force may explain part of the allocation inefficiencies that we found. Part of the systematic difference between marginal productivity and the wage rate is a return to the firm for the human capital accumulation it provides.

The food and mineral firms in the private sector have been found allocatively efficient yet the government firms were found more economically efficient. The ratio $\frac{A_g}{A_p}$ reported in Table 7 implies that technical advantages and other factors captured by the term A_{i0} are the main reasons why government firms appear to be slightly but significantly more economically efficient. Since many government firms are relatively new, they probably have newer vintages of capital. Furthermore, since a large part of the public firms used to be private, it is very probable that the government expropriated the most efficient firms in each industry. The size of the capital stock invested in the firm has been used as a criterion for nationalization. In developing economies it is reasonable to assume that efficiency is positively correlated with the size of a firm, therefore, nationalization resulted in the government sector absorbing the most efficient economic resources of the economy.

It is striking to observe that most of the highly educated labor at the level of chemists, engineers, and college-educated managers are employed in the public sector. For the period of 1962 - 1968, about 70 percent of the above group of labor is employed in government firms, while only 36 percent of the total manufacturing labor force is employed in the public sector. If these findings apply to the industries we studied, it will imply that we under-estimated the labor input used in the government firms by assuming that an hour of work in private and public firms are homogeneous. To answer this question we compared the product mix in the two sectors. It is apparent that industries such as sugar, electrical and machinery, ship building, printing and petroleum refineries are dominated completely by government ownership. Furthermore these industries were found to be the most human capital intensive industries in the industrial sector (skilled and technical labor in these industries amount to sixty to eighty percent of total labor). Since these industries are the cause of the high concentration of human capital in the public sector, we have no reason to suspect that we seriously underestimated the labor input used in the government firms that are included in this study.

An interesting result revealed in Tables 5, 6 and 7 is the signs of the technical change parameters λ_g^* and λ_p^*. Although their point estimates are not precise (they have large standard errors) they have striking similarity in the three industries: the sign of λ_g^* is always positive while λ_p^* is negative. No technological change took place in the private sector at the period studied. Most of the expropriations of private resources occurred in 1964. If indeed the government nationalized the most efficient firms, the technical change parameters may reflect mainly compositional change and not real technological change. This analysis is more relevant to the mineral and chemical industries in which significant change in ownership were observed during 1961 - 1967 (for example, all private cement firms were nationalized in 1964).

In the theoretical and empirical work presented in this chapter a production model and a distribution theory were combined together to study economic efficiency. To assess how reasonable our results had been, I tested the technical and allocative hypothesis in a non-joint model. Cobb-Douglas production functions were estimated with specific time and intercept coefficients for private and government firms. Using these estimates, marginal productivities were computed and compared to actual wages paid to labor. The results are completely in line with the evidence presented above. The government intercepts in the production functions were higher, the λ_g's were positive while the λ_p's negative. The ratios of computed marginal productivities to real wages were all higher than one, much more so for the government firms.

CHAPTER IV

CONCLUSIONS

In Chapter I we used the Divisia "residual" framework to study and quantify the contributions of the growth of capital, labor and factor productivity to the growth of the industrial sector in Iraq. The results obtained suggest that total factor productivity plays a moderate part in explaining the variation in the rate of output growth in the public sector in the period analyzed. Capital accumulation is the main vehicle to economic growth in Iraq: its growth accounts for 70 percent of output growth. The contribution of total labor accounts for 21 percent of output growth. Among the labor inputs, the group of skilled labor has made the largest contribution to growth. Surprising is the low contributions of the unskilled and technical labor groups (four and one percent, respectively).

The analyses for the sub-periods 1960-63 and 1964-67 reveal positive growth of factor productivity in the first period (the rate of growth is 1.4 percent per year) while no such growth is observed in the second period (the weighted contributions of inputs to the rate of growth of output leave no unexplained residual). Similar results are obtained for the private sector. Thus, it seems that the expropriation acts of 1964 disrupted production relationships in the economy and led to stagnation of factor productivity.

To obtain the average net rate of growth of total factor productivity, we computed average growth rates of output and inputs for the public sector net of the resources transferred from the private sector in 1964. The net rate of growth was found to be .512 percent, lower than the 1.79 gross rate. We concluded that a large part of the productivity in the years 1961-67 can be explained by the nationalization of the most productive private firms.

In Chapter II we developed a parametric approach to productivity measurement and applied it to the public manufacturing sector of Iraq. The empirical results indicate that productivity analyses are very sensitive to assumptions made regarding returns to scale and the form of technical change. The hypotheses of homotheticity, homogeneity and neutrality of technical change are all rejected for our data. The estimated annual rate of growth of total factor productivity in the model in accord with the data (non-homothetic, non-neutral technical change) is 1.3 percent. This figure is much lower than the rate obtained by the residual approach (1.8 percent).

A second important result obtained in Chapter II is the strong labor-saving bias in technical change. The labor bias parameters denoted by δ_{ti}, are all positive with high t-values. Labor-saving technical change affects negatively the demand for all kinds of labor. The demand elasticities, denoted by η_{ti} above, are similar for the unskilled, skilled and administrative groups but twice as large for technical labor. During the period of the analysis, all labor input-output coefficients declined. Part of this decline is a result of the fact that the private firms that were nationalized in 1964 were on average more capital intensive than the public firms. This can account for part of the decline since the labor input-output coefficients fell before 1964, and also over the entire period for the public sector net of the private resources that were nationalized.

Part of the reduction in these coefficients of all types of labor is explained by the strong labor-saving bias in technical change.

Technical labor, whose input-output coefficent show the sharpest decline, exhibits also the strongest labor saving bias estimated among the labor inputs.

The labor-saving results provide an explanation of the conflict between output and employment observed in many LDC's. This explanation was suggested before though no empirical evidence was provided. In the case of Iraq, since it does not have relatively abundant labor, labor-saving technical change may cause less severe employment problems than in other LDC's.

In Chapter III we analyzed relative economic efficiency of private and government firms in three industries in Iraq. Five hypotheses regarding allocative and technical efficiency were tested for each industry. The tests of equal relative economic efficiency reveal the interesting results that on the whole, government firms are more economically efficient than the private firms in the food and mineral industries, while in the chemical industry this equality is not rejected. Furthermore, the two kinds of firms differ significantly in the components of economic efficiency.

The joint hypothesis of equal allocative and technical efficiency is rejected for the three industries while the hypothesis of equal allocative efficiency is rejected for the food and mineral industries.

Examining the components of economic efficiency, sizeable allocation inefficiencies were found in the public firms: the ratio of value of marginal product to wages paid to labor ranges from 1.42 in the food industry to 2.51 in the chemical industry. On the other hand, we could not reject the hypothesis of optimal labor allocation in the private food and mineral firms. Yet we found that the government firms are more economically efficient. This results from these firms being more technically efficient, being able to produce more output with a given bundle of inputs. This technical advantage may very well be a consequence of the fact that the government managed to absorb the most productive resources in the economy. We found that most of the highly educated and trained labor force is employed in the public sector. We further established in Chapter I that the government nationalized the most productive private firms. Furthermore, since most of the investments in the industrial sector during the sixties were in the public sector, the new government plants had better vintages of capital. All these factors explain also why the time coefficients were all positive for the government firms, but negative for the private firms in all industries.

The results presented in Chapter III indicate that there seems to be significant possibilities for growth in Iraq by improving allocative efficiency in government firms and improving the technical efficiency of firms that do not belong to the public sector by moving them toward production frontiers.

APPENDIX

Data Description

This study makes use of information obtained from monthly, quarterly and annual industrial surveys of Iraq. We include in the analysis government's and private establishments employing ten or more employees.

The private and public manufacturing sectors together produce about ten percent of national GNP and employ 7-10 percent of the national labor force. The share of the sector in gross domestic fixed investment went up from seven percent in 1960 to 12 percent in 1969. The share of the public sector in total value added went up from ten percent in 1960 to 70 percent in 1968, after few nationalization acts during the 1960's.

TABLE 11

DEVELOPMENT OF RELATIVE WAGES IN IRAQ, 1961-1972

Year	$\frac{W^s}{W^u}$	$\frac{W^t}{W^u}$	$\frac{W^t}{W^s}$
1960	1.84	8.60	4.67
1961	1.72	8.30	4.83
1962	1.77	9.01	5.10
1963	1.82	8.72	4.80
1964	1.87	8.57	4.50
1965	2.06	8.43	4.10
1966	2.04	8.25	4.04
1967	1.99	7.73	3.87
1968	2.01	7.23	3.60
1972	2.00	3.29	1.65

Notes: W^u = wages of unskilled labor; W^s = wages of skilled labor; W^t = wages of technical labor (engineers, chemists, etc.)

The above table presents the development of relative wages in Iraq in 1960-1972. There is a clear tendency of a reduction in relative wages of the educated technical labor as compared with the two other labor groups.

The low rate of capital utilization observed in less developed countries makes it inappropriate to use the capital-services-proportional-to-capital-stock approach, since this approach does not take into account the degree of utilization of capital stock. In order to obtain a series that is expected to be closer to the "services" concept of capital utilization, we decided to use a series of energy consumption of the production units on this study. We assume that flow services of capital are produced through technical relationships that combine flow services of idle machines and flow of energy input. Recent studies of American and Canadian manufacturing technology (Berndt and Wood [1975], [1977]) have shown that capital and energy are complements in production in the strong definition of complementarity: σ_{KE}, the elasticity of substitution between capital and energy, is negative and high in absolute value. Moreover, the relationship with other factors of production is very similar for capital and energy. We thus assume that E and K are weakly separable from all other input in production. Furthermore, in view of the complementarity relation observed, we specify the technical relation that produces flow services of capital as a fixed proportion one, namely K and E are perfect complements:

$$KS = \text{Min}\ (K, E)$$

since in short-run production decisions, the energy component is the one which varies and reflects utilization degree, we therefore use it as an index for the flow services of capital.

The <u>Industrial Survey of Iraq</u>, published since 1954, gives details: average numbers of employers and workers, hours of work, wages and salaries, all detailed for the following groups:

Unskilled - includes those whose work does not need training or supervision;

Juveniles - includes children who are under 18 years of age;

Junior service personnel - includes those whose work do not have direct relation with the process of production, such as guards, waiters, etc.;

Skilled - those whose work needs experience and previous training;

Skilled technicals - includes those who supervise the process of production such as engineers, chemists, technical experts, etc.;

Administrative - directors of the establishment, accountants, clerks, etc.

We used hours of work as our labor input and no adjustment for quality has been made. The labor groups enter the production process as distinct input. Although we use a common unit of measurement, hours of work for each of them, we still treat them as different inputs, just as capital services and material inputs are distinct, although both are measured in real dollars. By adjusting for quality we will be making an assumption about degree of substitutability, something that we want to avoid.

In Chapter I all the six labor categories are used as distinct inputs in the Divisia index analyses of factor productivity. In Chapter II only four groups of labor are used in the econometric estimation. We make use of the Hicks composite good theorem to combine into one input the unskilled, juveniles and junior service labor, using their relative wages as weights. This step is made in order to avoid multicollinearity problems and to simplify the estimation procedures.

Wages for each type of labor are obtained by dividing the total payment to each group by its total hours of work. Variable profit is obtained by subtracting from value added all variable costs. The cost of energy inputs, electricity units bought from outside and fuel, are not subtracted since they are part of the cost of capital services as defined above.

The energy index, used as an index for the flow services of capital, is the consumption of energy in production measured in thousands of KWH. It includes electricity produced in the plant and bought from the electric company. This index has the advantage of reflecting directly the redistribution of capital from the private to the public sector as a result of nationalization. An attempt to estimate the government capital stock through a conventional perpetual inventory method is futile, since no data is available for the value of capital nationalized in 1961-1967 by the government.

The prices data are obtained from the national accounts of Iraq. The wholesale price index of manufacturing products is used to deflate the value added, variable profits and nominal wages used in the analyses of total factor productivity in Chapters I and II. Annual unit prices of food, mineral and chemical products are used in the empirical analyses of relative economic efficiency of private and government firms in these industries.

REFERENCES

Abramovitz, M. "Resource and Output Trends in the United States Since 1870." American Economic Review 46 (May 1956): 5-23.

Afriat, S. N. "Efficiency Estimation of Production Function." International Economic Review 13 (October 1972): 568-598.

Aigner, J. A. and Chu, S. F. "On Estimating Industry Production Functions." American Economic Review 58 (September 1968): 826-39.

Aigner, J.A.; Amemiya, T.; and Poirier, D. J. "On the Estimation of Production Frontiers." International Economic Review 17 (1976): 377-96.

Aigner, J.A.; Lovell, K.; and Schmidt, P. "Formulation and Estimation of Stochastic Frontier Production Function Models." Journal of Econometrics 6 (July 1977): 21-37.

Al-Dahiri, A. W. "The Introduction of Technology into Traditional Societies and Economies: Using Iraq as a Case Study." Al-Ani Press, 1969.

Allen, R. G. D. Mathematical Analyses for Economics. London: Macmillan, 1938.

Appblaum, E. "Testing Neoclassical Theory." Unpublished paper, University of Washington, August, 1976.

Atkinson, S. and Halvorsen, R. "Interfuel Substitution in Steam Electric Power Generation." Journal of Political Economy 84 (October 1976): 959-1013.

Berndt, E. R. and Christensen, L. R. "The Internal Structure of Functional Relationship: Separability, Substitution, and Aggregation." Review of Economic Studies 12 (July 1973): 403-10.

Berndt, E. R. and Savin, N. E. "Conflict among Criteria for Testing Hypotheses in the Multivariate Linear Regression Model." Econometrica 45 (July 1977): 1263-77.

Binswanger, H. "The Measurement of Technical Change Biases with Many Factors of Production." American Economic Review 64 (December 1974): 964-976.

Blackorby, C.; Lovell, C. A. Knox; and Thursby, M.C. "Extended Hicks Neutral Technical Change." Economic Journal 8 (December 1976): 845-52.

Bowles, S. "Aggregation of Labor Inputs in the Economics of Growth and Planning: Experiments with a Two-Level CES Function." Journal of Political Economy 78 (February 1970): 68-81.

Bruno, M. "Estimation of Factor Contribution to Growth under Structural Dis-equilibrium," International Economic Review (February 1968): 49-63.

Bruton, H. J. "Productivity Growth in Latin America." American Economic Review (December 1967): 1099-1116.

Christensen, L. R.; Jorgenson, D. W.; and Lau, L. J. "Transcendental Logarithmic Production Frontiers." Review of Economic Statistics 55 (February 1973): 28-45.

Correa, H. "Sources of Economic Growth in Latin America." Southern Economic Journal (July 1970): 17-31.

David, P. A. and Klundert, D. E. "Biased Efficiency Growth and Capital-Labor Substitution in the U.S." American Economic Review 55 (June 1965): 357-395.

Denison, E. Accounting for United States Economic Growth, 1929-1969. Washington, D. C.: The Brookings Institute.

__________. Why Growth Rates Differ. Washington, D. C.: The Brookings Institute, 1967.

Diewert, W. E. "Application of Duality Theory." In M. Intrilligator and D. Kendrick (eds.) Frontiers of Quantitative Economics. Amsterdam: North-Holland Publishing Co., 1974.

__________. "Functional Forms for Profit and Transformation Functions." Journal of Economic Theory 6 (April 1973): 284-316.

Dougherty, C. A. S. "Estimates of Labour Aggregation Functions." Journal of Political Economy 80 (December 1972): 1101-19.

Eckaus, R. S. "The Factor Proportions Problems in Underdeveloped Areas." American Economic Review 45 (September 1955): 539-65.

Fahim, I. Q. The Reconstruction of Iraq, 1950-1967. New York: Praeger Publishers, 1958.

Fallon, R. R. and Layard, P. R. G. "Capital-Skill Complementarity, Income Distribution, and Output Accounting." Journal of Political Economy 83 (April 1975): 279-301.

Farrell, M. J. "The Measurement of Productive Efficiency." Journal of the Royal Statistical Society 120 (1957): 253-82.

Gaathon, A. L. Capital Stock, Employment and Output in Israel, 1950-59. Jerusalem: Bank of Israel, 1961.

__________. Economic Productivity in Israel. New York: Praeger Publishers, 1971.

Griliches, Z. and Ringstad, V. Economies of Scale and the Form of the Production Function. Amsterdam: North-Holland Publishing Co., 1971.

Griliches, Z. "Capital-Skill Complementarity." Review of Economic Studies 51 (November 1969): 465-8.

Griliches, Z. "Notes on the Role of Education in Production Functions and Growth Accounting." In Education, Income and Human Capital. Edited by W. L. Hansen. New York: National Bureau of Economic Research, 1970.

Grossman, S. "Rational Expectations and the Econometric Modeling of Markets Subject to Uncertainty." Journal of Econometrics 3 (August 1975): 255-72.

Hanoch, G. "The Elasticity of Scale and the Shape of Average Costs." American Economic Review 3 (June 1975): 492-97.

Hoch, I. "Estimation of Production Function Parameters and Testing for Efficiency." Econometrica 23 (1955): 325-26.

__________. "Simultaneous Equation Bias in the Context of the Cobb-Douglas Production Function." Econometrica 26 (October 1958): 556-78.

Hopper, D. W. "Allocation Efficiency in a Traditional Agriculture." Journal of Farm Economics 47 (August 1965): 611-24.

International Bank for Reconstruction and Development. The Economic Development of Iraq. Baltimore: Johns Hopkins Press, 1952.

Jorgenson, E. and Griliches, Z. "The Explanation of Productivity Change." Review of Economic Statistics 34 (July 1967): 249-83.

Kmenta, J. and Gibbert, R. F. "Small Sample Properties and Alternative Estimators of Seemingly Unrelated Regressions." Journal of the American Statistical Association 63 (1968): 1180-1200.

Lau, L. J. "Applications of Profit Functions." Unpublished paper, Stanford University, March 1976. (a).

__________. "A Characterization of the Normalized Restricted Profit Function." Journal of Economic Theory 12 (February 1976): 131-63. (b).

__________. "Some Applications of Profit Functions." Memoranda 86A, 86B. Research Center for Economic Growth, Stanford University, November, 1969.

Lau, L. J. and Yotopoulos, P.A. "A Test for Relative Economic Efficiency: Some Further Results." American Economic Review 63 (March 1973): 214-23.

__________. "A Test for Relative Economic Efficiency and Application to Indian Agriculture." American Economic Review 61 (March 1971): 94-109.

McFadden, D. "Cost, Revenue, and Profit Functions: A Cursory Review." Working paper no. 86, Institute of Business and Economic Research, University of California Berkeley, 1966.

Morawetz, D. "Employment Implications of Industrialization in Developing Countries: A Survey." Economic Journal 84 (September 1974): 491-543.

Morawetz, D. "Economic Lessons from Some Small Socialist Developing Countries." Unpublished paper, 1977.

Mundlak, Y. "Estimation of Production and Behavioral Functions from a Combination of Cross-section and Time-series Data." In Christ, C. F. et al. Measurement in Economics. Stanford: Stanford University Press, 1963.

Muth, J. F. "Rational Expectations and the Theory of Price Movements." Econometrica 24 (July 1961): 315-35.

Nadiri, I. "Some Approaches to the Theory and Measurement of Total Factor Productivity: A Survey." Journal of Economic Literature (1970): 1137-78.

Richmond, J. "Estimating the Efficiency of Production." International Economic Review 15 (June 1974): 515-21.

Salter, L. "The Development of Iraq." Iraq Development Board, 1955.

Sato, R. "The Estimation of Biased Technical Progress and Production Functions." International Economic Review 11 (June 1970): 179-208.

Schmidt, P. "On the Statistical Estimation of Parametric Production Functions." Review of Economic Statistics 58 (May 1976): 238-9.

Schultz, T. W. Transforming Traditional Agriculture. New Haven: Yale University Press, 1964.

Sidhu, S. S. "Relative Efficiency in Wheat Production in the Indian Punjab." American Economic Review 64 (September 1974): 742-51.

Solow, R. M. "Technical Change and the Aggregate Production Function." Review of Economic Statistics 39 (1959): 312-20.

Star, S. "Accounting for the Growth of Output." American Economic Review 64 (1974): 123-35.

Stewart, F. and Streeter, P. "Conflicts between Output and Employment in LDC's." Oxford Economic Papers 23 (July 1971): 145-68.

Theil, H. Principles of Econometrics. Toronto: John Wiley & Sons, 1971.

Timmer, C. "Using a Probabilistic Frontier Production Function to Measure Technical Efficiency." Journal of Political Economy 79 (July 1971): 776-94.

Turnham, D. The Employment Problem in Less Developed Countries. Paris: Organization of Economic Development and Cooperation, 1971.

United Nations Studies on Selected Development Problems in Various Countries in the Middle East. "Manpower and Employment Planning in Iraq and the Syrian Arab Republic." (1975): 22-45.

United Nations Studies on Selected Development Problems in Various Countries in the Middle East. "Trial Application of Multisectoral Analyses and Projections: Case Studies of Jordan and Iraq." (1970): 33-71.

__________. "Plan Implementation in Iraq, 1951-1967." (1969): 1-19.

__________. "Plan Formulation and Development in Iraq." (1968): 1-11. (a).

__________. "Some Aspects of the Development of Human Resources in Various Countries of the Middle East." (1968): 35-47. (b).

__________. "An Analysis of Development Plans in Various Countries in the Middle East." (1962): 1-13.

Uzawa, H. "Production Functions with Constant Elasticities of Substitution." Review of Economic Studies 44 (October 1962): 291-99.

Welch, F. "Education in Production." Journal of Political Economy 78 (February 1970): 35-59.

Williamson, J. G. "Dimensions of Philippine Postwar Economic Progress." Quarterly Journal of Economics (February 1969):

__________. "Relative Price Changes, Adjustment Dynamics and Productivity Growth: The Case of Philippine Manufacturing." Economic Development and Cultural Change (July 1971):

Wise, J. and Yotopoulos P. A. "The Empirical Content of Rationality: A Test for a Less Developed Economy." Journal of Political Economy 77 (December 1969): 976-1004.

Wymer, C. R. "Computer Programs: RESIMUL Manual." London School of Economics, 1973.

Zellner, A. "An Efficient Method of Estimating Seemingly Unrelated Regressions and Tests for Aggregation." Journal of the American Statistical Association 57 (June 1962): 348-68.

Zellner, A.; Kmenta, J.; and Dreze, J. "Specification and Estimation of Cobb-Douglas Production Function Models." Econometrica 34 (October 1966): 784-95.